Quick Quilts
Using Quick Bias

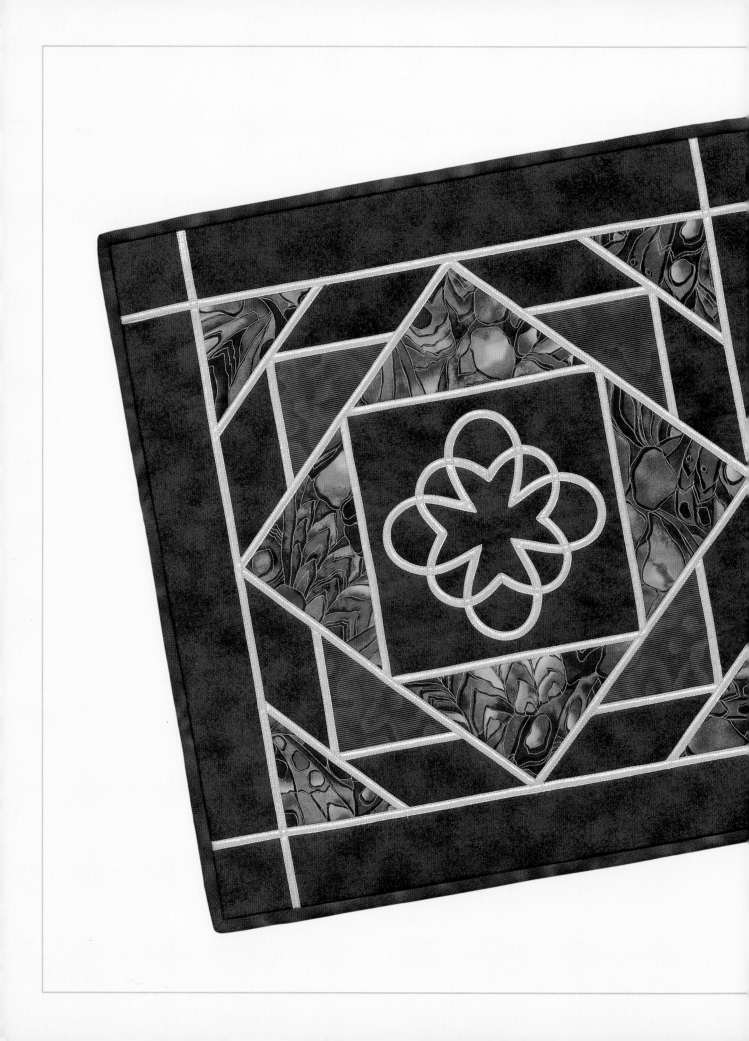

Quick Quilts
Using Quick Bias

Gretchen K. Hudock

Martingale™
& COMPANY

Credits

President	Nancy J. Martin
CEO	Daniel J. Martin
Publisher	Jane Hamada
Editorial Director	Mary V. Green
Managing Editor	Tina Cook
Technical Editor	Laurie Baker
Copy Editor	Allison A. Merrill
Design Director	Stan Green
Illustrator	Laurel Strand
Cover and Text Designer	Regina Girard
Photographer	Brent Kane

Martingale™
& C O M P A N Y

That
Patchwork
Place®

That Patchwork Place® is an imprint
of Martingale & Company™.

Quick Quilts Using Quick Bias
© 2002 by Gretchen K. Hudock

Martingale & Company
20205 144th Avenue NE
Woodinville, WA 98072-8478 USA
www.martingale-pub.com

Printed in China
07 06 05 04 03   8 7 6 5 4 3

Mission Statement

We are dedicated to providing quality products and service by working together to inspire creativity and to enrich the lives we touch.

Library of Congress Cataloging-in-Publication Data
Hudock, Gretchen K.
    Quick quilts using Quick Bias / Gretchen K. Hudock.
        p. cm.
    ISBN 1-56477-429-5
    1. Quilting—Patterns. 2. Quilting—Equipment and supplies. I. Title.
TT835 .H789 2002
746.46' 041—dc21   2002007494

Dedication

To my family: Rich, John, and Elizabeth

Acknowledgments

Thank you to:

Sue Petruske and Kate Bashynski for testing the quilt patterns
and giving welcome improvements.

Merry Anderson and Kate Bashynski for being creative
with the project names.

Laure Noe for her ability to illustrate with ease.

Mary Kotek for her beautiful hand quilting and editing expertise.

Jan Carr from Clover for allowing me to experiment and
create quilts using Quick Bias in new applications.

Martingale & Company for making it possible
for me to share my designs.

A big thank-you to my coworkers for their support
and encouragement as I worked on the book.

And special thanks to my husband, Rich, for his patience
and understanding during the production of the book.

Contents

Introduction

With the invention of Quick Bias, a pre-folded, fusible bias tape manufactured by Clover, a new world of creativity opened for quilters and sewers. Stained glass quilts are now much easier to make, and curved embellishments on garments are simplified. This book will show you just a few ways you can use this timesaving notion to make fabulous quilts.

Using Quick Bias doesn't require much time or effort (hence the name), but there are some basic techniques that you'll need to be familiar with to complete the projects in this book. You'll find everything you need to know in "Quick Bias Quilt Basics" starting on page 11.

The remainder of the book is devoted to the ten projects. You'll find complete instructions and helpful illustrations to complete a variety of home accessories, table toppers, and wall quilts. Keep in mind that the projects are given in order of difficulty, so you may want to warm up with "Lattice Memories" (page 30) or "Tic-Tac-Toe Twist" (page 33) before tackling the intricacies of "Woven Trellis" (page 72). As you make each project, you will also learn new techniques. Make the project and learn the associated technique; then use the technique in other projects from the book or in projects you design yourself.

Each of the projects uses no more than one 11-yard spool of ¼"-wide Quick Bias. Many quilt shops now carry Quick Bias, but if you have trouble finding it, check "Resources" on page 78 for mail-order information. Quick Bias is available in a variety of colors, so matching your decor shouldn't be a problem. All the projects in this book were created with purchased Quick Bias, but Clover also offers products for making your own fusible bias tape.

Although the projects in this book are quilts, the possibilities for Quick Bias are limitless. I hope this book will inspire you to use it to create your own designs for yourself and others. Enjoy exploring new ways to use Quick Bias—you may be opening a new chapter in your quilting and sewing!

Quick Bias Quilt Basics

The basics are always important in learning new techniques. Take some time to read the following guidelines—they could save you from having to "reverse sew" later. Now let's get started.

Gathering Your Supplies

All of the items needed to make the projects in this book should be readily available at your local fabric store or quilt shop; if not, see "Resources" on page 78.

Quick Bias. This ready-to-use bias tape comes in spools of 5½ yards and 11 yards. Refer to the project materials list for the approximate amount needed. Use the ¼"  width for all of the projects in this book. Quick Bias comes in a wide range of colors and is 100 percent cotton (except for the metallic tapes, which are 100 percent polyester). A strip of fusible web is centered on the back of the tape but does not extend to its edges, making it possible to stitch the tape down along its edges without gumming up your needle. Quick Bias is washable and dry-cleanable.

Fabric. The best choice of fabric for these projects is 100 percent cotton. Cotton blends and other fibers may not be able to withstand the heat needed to apply Quick Bias correctly. Textured solids, batiks, and marbled fabrics work very well. Prints, including stained glass prints and prints of small to medium scale, can also be used, but be sure the fabric you choose does not overpower the bias tape. For this reason and because of the small size of the finished projects, avoid large-scale prints.

Yardage requirements are based on 42" of usable fabric after preshrinking. Apply spray-on fabric starch to replace body lost during washing, and press your fabrics before you begin.

Paper. Use plain white copy paper or semi-transparent paper for tracing the designs from the book.

Nonpermanent pencil or fabric marker, or carbonless transfer paper and transfer wheel. The tool you should use for transferring the design to the fabric depends on the method you choose (see "Transferring the Design to the Base Material" on page 12). The marking tools I prefer include a water-soluble marker for light-color fabrics and a soapstone marker for dark-color fabrics. Marks made with these products are easily removed if you need to correct a mistake.

Gridded fusible interfacing with 1" grid marks. This product is required for the projects "Crown Jewel" (page 43) and "Woven Trellis" (page 72).

Sew-through paper-backed fusible web or temporary spray adhesive. You will need one of these products to apply pieces of fabric to the base material.

Batting. Choose low-loft cotton, cotton-polyester, or polyester batting for these projects. I prefer a dense, low-loft, needle-punched polyester batting because it provides stability, especially for wall quilts. Avoid high-loft battings. The loftier the batting, the more difficult it is to apply and stitch down Quick Bias.

Sewing-machine needles. A size 80/12 universal needle is suitable for almost all of the required stitching. The stitching performs two functions at the same time: quilting and attaching the Quick Bias, so a smaller needle is not recommended. A 4.0/90 double needle can be used to stitch down both edges of the tape at the same time on straight areas or on very gently curved areas, but it does not work well on sharp curves. A size 80/12 metallic or machine embroidery needle can be used when working with specialty threads, if necessary, to achieve a balanced stitch.

Thread. Use thread in a color that matches your Quick Bias when stitching it down. Cotton, rayon, metallic, or monofilament thread may be used, but in most cases a 50-weight cotton works best. Choose a heavier thread (the number will be smaller) for a more pronounced look. Bobbin thread should match the top thread—even if you're using a lighter-weight thread in the bobbin. This will prevent the bobbin thread from showing in case the tension of your machine is not perfect.

Mini-iron or conventional iron. A mini-iron's small heated surface is ideal for fusing Quick Bias into place, and it is easier to manipulate than a conventional iron.

Stiletto. Use this tool to shape the bias tape around corners and angles.

Portable pressing surface. A small pressing surface makes it easier to turn the project while applying Quick Bias.

Rotary cutting equipment. Use a rotary cutter, ruler, and mat for normal cutting tasks, and a rotary ruler for applying bias tape along straight areas.

Transferring the Design to the Base Material

The first step in making one of these projects is to transfer the design to the base material. This transferred design will help you position the fabric pieces and Quick Bias. (See "Making Your Own Quick Bias Designs" on page 14 for products you may want to use in making your own designs.) Because the designs for the projects in this book are too large to be shown complete, an eighth, quarter, or half of the design may be given, or you may be required to enlarge the design on a photocopy machine. Reposition the base material or the pattern (depending on the transfer method you choose) to complete the transfer of the design.

Choose from three methods for transferring the design to the base material. In methods I and II, fabric is used as the base. In method I you place the pattern under the base fabric, while in method II you place the pattern over the base fabric. "Crown Jewel" (page 43) and "Woven Trellis" (page 72) utilize method III (see those projects for instructions), in which the design is transferred to a base of gridded fusible interfacing rather than fabric. Method III works well for any straight-line design because the printed grid helps you transfer the design; you may even be able to use the grid itself as your pattern. If you do not have access to gridded fusible interfacing, you can draw your own grid on the smooth side of lightweight fusible interfacing with a fine-point marker.

Method I

1. Photocopy the pattern for the desired project from the book, or trace the pattern onto a piece of paper. Be sure to include all lines. Solid lines indicate placement for fabric pieces and Quick Bias; dashed lines are for alignment purposes.
2. Fold the base fabric in half lengthwise and widthwise, and gently press the folds. The resulting creases will help you align the pattern and fabric.

3. Tape the photocopied or traced pattern to a light source. A light box or a window both work well. Or, place a light under a plastic table extension for a sewing machine. If you have a table you can pull apart to insert extension leaves, place a sheet of glass over the opening and put a lamp underneath (remove the shade).

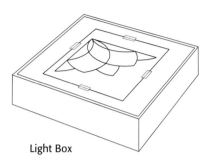

Light Box

4. Place the base fabric right side up over the pattern, aligning the creases on the fabric with the corresponding lines on the pattern. Tape down the edges of the fabric just enough to keep it from shifting while tracing but not enough to make it difficult to remove when you need to reposition the fabric. Using a nonpermanent pencil or fabric marker, trace the design onto the fabric. Use a clear acrylic ruler to trace straight lines accurately. Once you have traced the portion of the design contained on the pattern, rotate the fabric to trace the next portion. Align the lines on the pattern with the creases on the fabric after each rotation. Refer to the project instructions and the diagram given with each design for additional guidance.

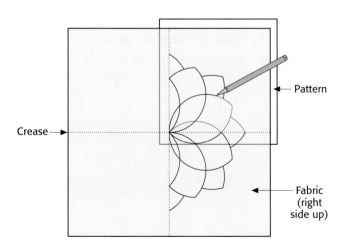

Crease

Pattern

Fabric (right side up)

Method II

1. Follow steps 1 and 2 of method I.
2. Lay the base fabric right side up on a flat surface. Tape it in place around the edges, using just enough tape so the fabric doesn't shift.
3. Place a sheet of carbonless transfer paper, transfer side down, over the fabric.
4. Place the traced pattern over the fabric and transfer paper, aligning the creases on the fabric with the corresponding lines on the pattern. Tape the pattern in place, using just enough tape to keep the pattern from shifting while tracing but not enough to make it difficult to remove when you need to reposition the pattern. Using a tracing wheel, trace over the design to transfer it to the fabric. Once you have traced the portion of the design contained on the pattern, rotate the pattern and transfer paper to trace the next portion. Align the lines on the pattern with the creases on the fabric after each rotation. Refer to the project instructions and the diagram given with each design for additional guidance.

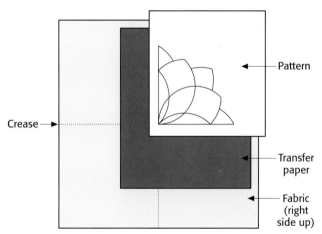

Crease

Pattern

Transfer paper

Fabric (right side up)

Making Your Own Quick Bias Designs

Once you find out how easy it is to work with Quick Bias, you'll want to use it on all sorts of projects. Inspirations for creating your own designs are endless, but there are several products that make it really easy.

Quilting stencils are abundant and are ideal for use in Quick Bias projects. Continuous-line stencils are especially good because you can apply the bias tape in one piece and not have to start and stop several times. Choose stencils that do not have tight curves (there are ways to handle sharp corners, but it is difficult to apply Quick Bias smoothly to a tight curve). If the stencil design is the correct size for your project, place it on the base fabric where desired and mark it with your favorite marking tool. If the stencil is not the size you need, draw the stencil design on paper and reduce or enlarge it on a photocopy machine. Then transfer the design to the base fabric, using either method I or method II.

Several companies sell preprinted paper stencils that are applied directly to the fabric and then torn away after they are stitched. Quick Bias is then applied over the stitching lines. If you use a tear-away stencil, you can layer your quilt with batting and backing before stitching the design, or you can simply stitch through the stencil paper and base fabric to mark it before layering. A tear-away stabilizer placed under your fabric while stitching will help avoid puckers if you choose the latter method.

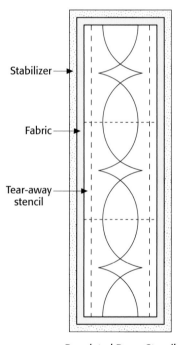

Preprinted Paper Stencil

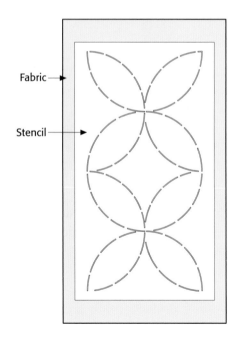

Applying Fabric to the Marked Design

The next step is to add any fabric pieces to the base. In this book, all of the projects except "I'm Bias for Spiders" incorporate fabric pieces. If you are creating your own designs from stencils, consider adding fabric in some of the sections and outlining them with bias tape rather than just using bias tape alone.

Fabrics are applied to the base material temporarily and then stitched down permanently when the bias tape is applied. If your design has been traced onto fabric, you can use either paper-backed fusible web or temporary spray adhesive to hold the fabric pieces in place. Adhesive spray gives a softer appearance to the finished quilt, but there is less likelihood of the pieces shifting while they are being stitched down if you use fusible web. If your design has been created on gridded fusible interfacing, follow the project instructions to press the fabric pieces onto the fusible side of the interfacing to hold them in place temporarily.

Fusible-Web Method

1. Using the patterns indicated for the design, trace the required number of each shape onto the paper side of a sew-through paper-backed fusible web, leaving a small amount of space between the pieces. There is no need to make a mirror image of any of the pieces used for the designs in this book. Be as accurate as possible when tracing. To save time, group like pieces together. In other words, if you need 8 each of pieces A and B, trace all 8 A pieces in one section and all 8 B pieces in another section. If you trace pieces in a group, try to keep them oriented in the same direction so

they can all be placed on the straight of grain when they are fused to the fabric.

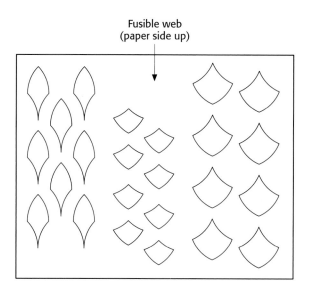

Fusible web
(paper side up)

2. Roughly cut around each individual shape, or if there are several of the same shape, cut around each group.

3. Follow the manufacturer's instructions to fuse the traced shapes to the wrong side of the appropriate fabric. Try to position the shapes so they will be cut on the straight grain whenever

possible. Let cool. Cut out each individual shape along the drawn lines, and remove the paper backing.

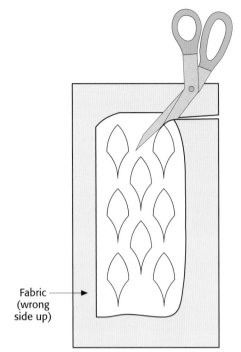

Fabric
(wrong
side up)

4. Follow the project instructions to place the pieces on the base fabric in the appropriate positions. Place the pieces next to each other so that none of the base fabric is visible. Once you are pleased with the placement, follow the manufacturer's instructions to fuse the pieces in place.

Temporary Spray Adhesive Method

1. Trace one of each of the patterns indicated for the desired project onto paper to make a template (only one of each pattern is needed because the template can be used multiple times). The type of paper does not matter, but I like to use a gridded iron-on paper because it helps me align my templates on the straight of grain, and also eliminates pinning the template to the fabric while cutting.

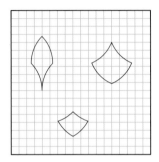

2. For each template, cut a piece of fabric slightly larger than the template from the appropriate fabric(s). If you will be cutting more than one fabric piece using the same template, even if they are from different fabrics, cut the desired number of fabric pieces and stack them together, right sides up. Pin or iron the template to the top fabric piece. Be careful not to overpress if you are using iron-on paper templates. Cut out the fabric pieces. Cut out as many pieces at once as you are comfortable cutting, reusing the template as necessary.

Fabric pieces
(right side up)

3. Place one of the fabric pieces on a piece of scrap paper, wrong side up. Follow the manufacturer's instructions to spray the fabric piece's wrong side with adhesive. Place the fabric piece, adhesive side down, onto the base fabric in the appropriate position. Repeat to apply the remaining fabric pieces to the design. If pieces butt up next to each other, place the pieces so that none of the base is visible. If desired, use straight pins to hold the pieces down more securely.

Assembling the Project Layers

For most of the projects, the next step is to prepare the project for quilting by assembling the top, batting, and backing layers. This will seem out of sequence for those who are familiar with traditional quilting, but for most Quick Bias projects it is possible to machine stitch the bias tape in place and do the quilting at the same time. What a time-saver! There are some exceptions to this sequence, however, so be sure to follow the project instructions. Be aware that if you choose to hand stitch Quick Bias in place after it has been fused, you will definitely want to do the stitching before you do the layering, to avoid working with the additional bulk. Unless specifically stated, the instructions are written

assuming you are machine stitching, so make changes accordingly for hand stitching. You should also note that the borders are sometimes added before the project is layered and sometimes after it is layered. I will discuss different border applications under "Borders" on page 23.

To assemble the layers:

1. Lay the backing, wrong side up, on a flat work surface. Smooth out any wrinkles and secure it to the work surface by applying masking tape around all of the edges. Apply the tape to opposite sides first, then the remaining two sides, and finally the corners. Continue rearranging the tape until the backing is smooth and taut.
2. Place batting over the backing and smooth out any wrinkles.
3. Center the base fabric with the fused fabric pieces right side up over the batting. Smooth out any wrinkles. You may be adding borders to the quilt top later, so do not be alarmed if there is an excessive margin of batting and backing around the top, and do not trim it away.
4. Pin-baste the layers together with size 1 rust-proof safety pins. Avoid placing pins in areas where Quick Bias will be applied.

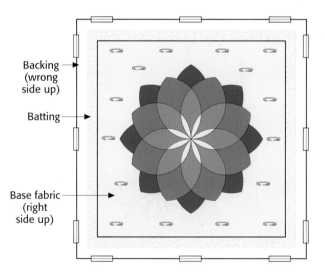

Backing (wrong side up)

Batting

Base fabric (right side up)

Applying the Quick Bias

Now it's time to apply the Quick Bias to the design lines. Each piece will be fused in place first and then stitched down by hand or machine, whichever you prefer, before the next piece is added, unless otherwise noted in the project instructions.

1. Set your iron on a cotton setting if you are working with cotton bias tape (high setting on the mini-iron); use a slightly cooler temperature for metallic bias tape. If you are using a conventional iron, you will not need steam. Check to see how long it takes to fuse the tape in place and to be sure the iron temperature is correct by fusing a small piece of Quick Bias to a scrap of the base fabric. Adjust the temperature and pressing time if necessary.

Tip

When applying Quick Bias to long, straight edges, use a rotary ruler as a guide. Place the ruler edge parallel to the straight edge of the design, leaving enough room for the tape to be centered over the line. Place the edge of the tape parallel to the ruler and guide the iron along it. Being able to see through the ruler will help you keep lines parallel.

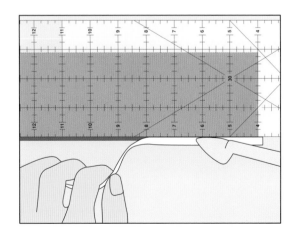

2. Refer to the project instructions for any special sequence in which the tape should be applied. If no special order is indicated, or if you are working with your own design, plan the sequence so that the ends of each strip are covered by other strips or extend beyond the base and are enclosed in a border or binding seam. This is extremely important for a clean look. If you are using a continuous-line design, you will use only one strip of tape, beginning and ending at the same point. Plan this point to be at an intersection where another piece will cross over the join and hide it.

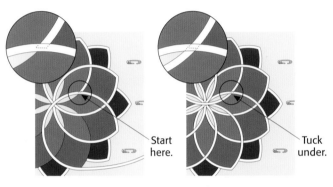

Start here.   Tuck under.

Continuous-Line Design

In some instances, such as with a circle, you will need to turn under one end and overlap it with the other end (see "Floral-Go-Round" on page 48). Refer to "Achieving the Celtic Look" on page 21 for planning the over-and-under sequence of Celtic designs.

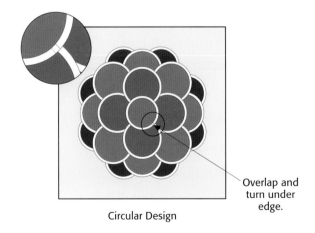

Overlap and turn under edge.

Circular Design

3. Place the project on the portable pressing surface. Peel off approximately the first 12" of the paper backing from the Quick Bias. (The backing will not adhere to the tape again once it is removed, so remove the backing only as you work.) With the end at the determined beginning point, center the Quick Bias over the design line. Be sure to place the end so that it will be completely covered by the strip that crosses over it. If two pieces of fabric are butted together covering the design line, center the tape over the butted edges.

4. Fuse the first piece of tape into place, following the sequence determined previously. Hold the iron in your dominant hand and the tape in the other. If you are right-handed, begin at the starting point and work toward the left of the project. If you are left-handed, work toward the right of the project. Remove the paper backing as you go, and be careful not to stretch the tape as you apply it. Turn the pressing surface as needed to keep the work area in front of you.

You will need either to miter or to overlap the tape at corners. For angles 90° or greater, miter the tape. For angles less than 90°, overlap the tape.

For a mitered corner, apply Quick Bias up to the point of the angle. Place the tip of a stiletto over the tape at the point of the angle as shown. Turn the tape to begin applying the next side, but do not press it into place yet. Slowly turn the stiletto tip toward the unpressed tape, stopping when a miter is formed. Press the mitered corner and next edge in place.

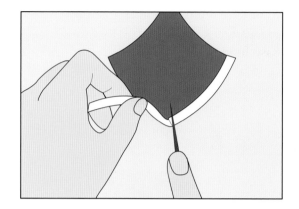

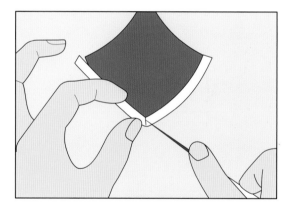

Mitered Corner

For an overlapped corner, apply Quick Bias up to the point of the angle. Place the stiletto tip over the tape at the point of the angle as shown. Turn the tape to begin applying the next side, but do not press it into place yet. Slowly turn the stiletto tip toward the unpressed edge so that the tape folds over the tip. Bring the fold to the outer edge of the previously pressed-down edge, and press it into place.

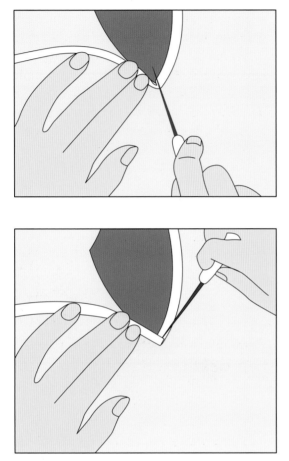

Overlapped Corner

5. Check the fused tape for any mistakes in following the design. If you find an area that needs to be redone, place the iron over the area to loosen the adhesive, lift the Quick Bias up, reposition it, and press it back in place. The adhesive will lose some bonding power each time this is done, so be careful not to loosen the same area more than absolutely necessary.

6. Set your machine for a short stitch length, approximately 12 to 15 stitches per inch. This will enable you to stitch the tape effectively on curves. Use the needle-down feature if your machine has one. A straight-stitch presser foot can be used, but it may be difficult to see where you are stitching. An open-toe foot allows you a clear field of vision. An edge-joining foot works well because the guide runs along the edge of the tape to help you stitch accurately; set your needle so it will stitch along the edge of the tape.

Straight-Stitch Foot   Open-Toe Foot

Edge-Joining Foot

7. Stitch the Quick Bias to the project, using one of the options listed in "Stitch Options" on page 22. Begin and end the line of stitching with tiny stitches to lock them in place.

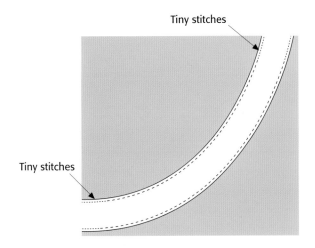

Tiny stitches

Tiny stitches

8. Continue fusing and stitching the Quick Bias to the design lines until the design is complete.

Achieving the Celtic Look

It's easy to achieve the traditional over-and-under look of Celtic designs with Quick Bias. Just apply the tape as you would for a continuous-line design, always crossing the tape over any previously applied tape as you come to it. Do not worry about whether the strip should be over or under another strip at this time. Lightly press the tapes together at intersections. After the design is complete, plan your over-and-under sequence. For intersections where the strip on top should be on the bottom, warm the area with the iron to loosen the adhesive bond, carefully cut the top strip at the center of the overlap, and tuck the ends under the bottom piece. Re-press the intersection.

Cut.

Tuck under.

Topstitch

Stitch as close to the edge of the tape as possible. A slow machine speed and small stitches will help you be accurate. Once you have stitched one side of the tape, stitch the other side either by moving the needle position or by turning the project around. If your design is made up of straight and/or very gently curving lines, you can also use a 4.0/90 double needle to stitch both edges at once.

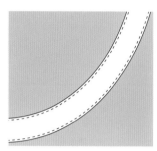

Topstitch

Blind Hem Stitch

For a hand-stitched look done by machine, use the blind hem stitch. Position the needle so that the straight part of the stitch runs along the outside edge of the tape and the "bite" catches just a couple of threads of the tape. Stitch one side of the tape; then turn the project and stitch the other.

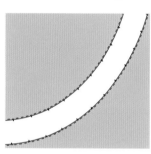

Blind Hem Stitch

Decorative Stitches

One of your machine's decorative stitches can secure the tape quickly and add textural interest. The featherstitch usually works well. Experiment with stitch width to find one that will cover the entire width of the tape in one pass instead of two. This method is especially attractive with metallic thread on metallic Quick Bias.

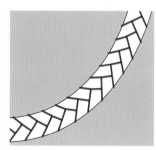

Decorative Stitch

Hand Appliqué Stitch

Quick Bias can be permanently secured with a hand appliqué stitch, but this should be done before the project top is layered with batting and backing. Choose this method if you prefer handwork or if you are intimidated by machine stitching close to the edge of the tape. The great advantage of hand stitching is that it enables you to control both the stitching and the tape completely. The tape responds well to slight easing as you negotiate tight curves. Use an appliqué needle and thread that matches the color of the tape. Use tiny, hidden stitches for a beautifully flat and smooth finish that gives a free-floating, three-dimensional look to your finished project. When you are finished stitching down the tape, layer the project top with batting and backing as described in "Assembling the Project Layers" on page 17. Hand or machine quilt as desired to secure the layers.

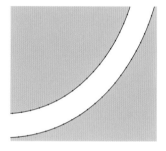

Hand Appliqué Stitch

Finishing Your Project

Borders

Borders are added to most of the projects in this book with either a variation on the traditional method or the Quick Bias method. Refer to the project instructions for when to add the borders and for which method to use.

Traditional Variation Method

1. Check the border markings to be sure they are still straight and have not shifted during stitching; re-mark the lines if necessary.

2. Measure the quilt top through its vertical center. Cut the side borders to that length and to the width indicated in the project instructions. With right sides together, place the side borders on the quilt top, aligning the edge of the border with the marked lines as shown. Stitch the side borders in place through all of the layers, using a ¼" seam allowance.

3. Trim the background fabric seam allowance to ¼". Do not trim the batting and backing at this time. From the right side of the quilt top, press the borders out.

4. Measure the quilt top through its horizontal center, including the side borders. Cut the top and bottom borders to that length and to the width indicated in the project instructions. Stitch the borders to the top and bottom edges of the quilt in the same manner as the side borders.

5. Trim the backing and batting even with the edges of the quilt top, and finish the borders as desired or as indicated in the project instructions.

Quick Bias Method

1. Check the border markings to be sure they are still straight and have not shifted during stitching; re-mark the lines if necessary.

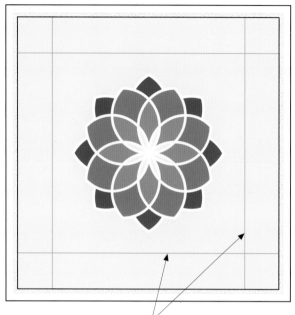

Check border markings for accuracy.

2. Apply fusible web or temporary spray adhesive to the wrong side of the border strips. Position the borders, right side up, so the border inner edges meet the marked border line on the quilt top. Fuse or press the borders in place.

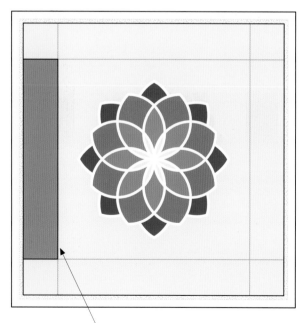

Butt border edge to marked border line.

3. Refer to "Applying the Quick Bias" on page 18 to fuse and stitch Quick Bias over the horizontal border lines and then the vertical border lines to cover the raw edges of the fabric. Use a ruler to keep the Quick Bias straight while you fuse it in place (see page 18).

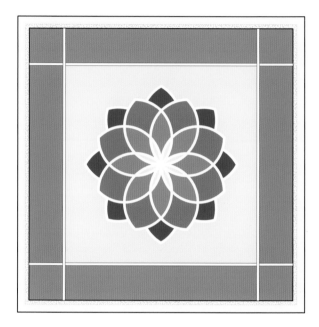

4. Trim the backing and batting even with the edges of the quilt top, and finish the borders as desired or as indicated in the project instructions.

French Twist Binding

The French twist binding method is a variation on the commonly used French binding method. By increasing the width of the strips to 5" and folding the excess to the back of the quilt, two pockets are formed in which you can insert a hanging rod. By extending the binding onto the quilt back instead of stitching it down at the seam line, the quilt edges are more stable and the quilt hangs better.

1. Join the binding strips into one long, continuous strip using diagonal seams. Trim ¼" from the seam line and press the seam allowance open.

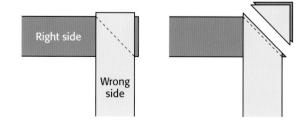

Right side

Wrong side

2. Trim one end of the strip at a 45° angle.

3. Fold the binding strip in half lengthwise, wrong sides together.

4. Using straight pins, pin the quilt layers together around the outer edges. Beginning with the angled end, place the binding strip approximately two-thirds of the way down one edge of the right side of the quilt top. Align the quilt top and binding raw edges. Leaving the first 6" of the binding unstitched, stitch the binding to the quilt. Use a ¼" seam allowance. Stop stitching ¼" from the corner. Backstitch and remove the quilt from the machine.

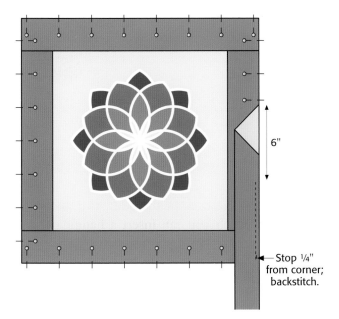

6"

Stop ¼" from corner; backstitch.

5. Turn the project so you are ready to sew the next side. Fold the binding up so it creates a 45° angle.

6. Fold the binding back down so the new fold is even with the top edge of the quilt and the binding raw edge is aligned with the side of the quilt. Make sure the binding is relaxed on the quilt; do not pull too tight or the binding will pucker. Beginning at the fold, stitch the binding to the quilt, stopping ¼" from the next corner. Repeat the folding and stitching process for each corner.

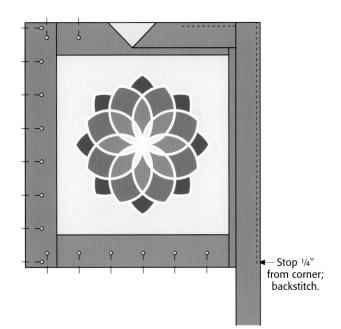

Stop ¼" from corner; backstitch.

7. When you are approximately 6" from the starting point, stop stitching and remove the quilt from the machine. Lay the beginning tail on the quilt top, aligning the raw edges with the quilt top. Lay the ending tail over the beginning tail. Cut the ending tail approximately 2" longer than needed.

8. Place the beginning tail inside the ending tail. Make 2 marks on the ending tail to indicate the angled edges of the beginning tail.

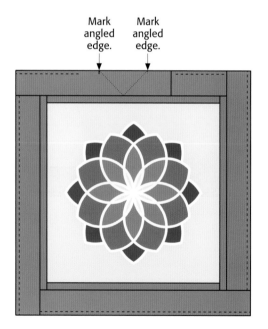

9. Remove the beginning tail from the ending tail. Open up the ending tail so it lies flat with the wrong side up. Mark a diagonal line on the ending tail, connecting the two marked points. Measure ½" to the right of the marked line and mark another line. Trim the excess ending tail along the second marked line.

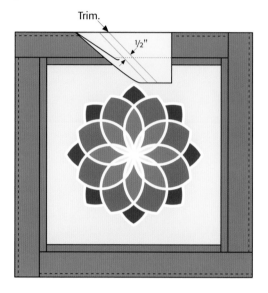

10. Place the beginning and ending tails right sides together with raw edges aligned. A small triangle of fabric will extend beyond each end. Stitch the ends together, using a ¼" seam allowance. Press the seam allowance open.

11. Refold the binding. Finish stitching the binding to the edge of the quilt top.

12. Remove the straight pins. Press the binding away from the quilt top.
13. Fold the binding on the sides of the quilt to the back, and pin it in place.

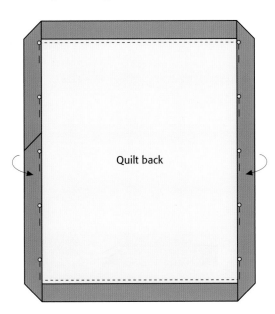

14. Fold the binding on the top and bottom of the quilt to the back, and pin it in place. Adjust the corners so the binding forms a miter on the front of the quilt and overlaps on the back of the quilt.

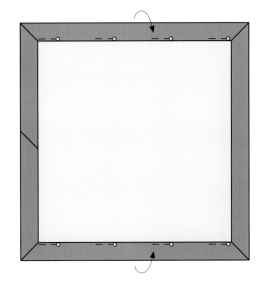

15. From the front of the quilt, stitch in the ditch along the binding seam line.

16. From the quilt back, slipstitch the binding to the quilt backing along the fold. Do not stitch down the corners. This forms a rod pocket at the top and bottom edges of your quilt.

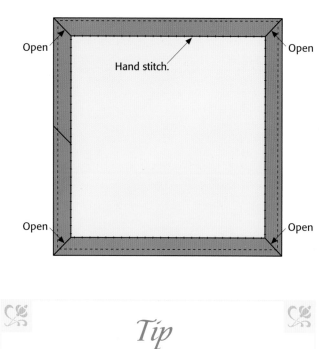

Tip

I use fiberglass rods meant for electric fence posts, which I purchase at farm-supply stores, to hang my quilts. They are heavier than wooden dowels, will not warp, and are cut easily with a fine-tooth saw. Measure the quilt between the border stitch-in-the-ditch lines, and cut two rods to that size. Then insert them through the pockets at the top and bottom and rest the top rod on two nails in the wall.

Envelope Pillow Backing

If you prefer to finish your project as a pillow cover rather than as a quilt, this method is my favorite because there is no hand stitching needed. An added benefit is that the pillow form is easily removed when you want to launder the cover. If your project does not fit a ready-made pillow form, make your own by stuffing a muslin shell the size of your project with polyester fiberfill.

For quilt tops that measure 16" x 16" or smaller:
1. Stitch a scant ¼" from the outside edges of the quilt top.
2. Working on the back of the quilt top, measure through the horizontal center. Add 2" to this measurement. Cut a piece of fabric 42" long and the determined width. Cut this piece in half widthwise. Press each of the pieces in half widthwise, wrong sides together. These will be the pillow back pieces.

Measure.

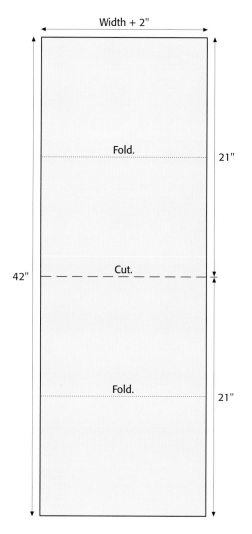

3. With right sides together, pin the pillow back pieces to the quilt top, overlapping the folds in the center of the top by 4". The back pieces will extend beyond the edges of the quilt top. Pin the back pieces in place.

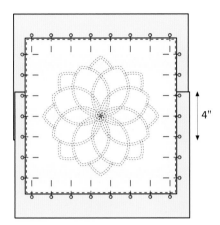

4. Stitch the back pieces to the quilt top, following the stitching lines from step 1. Stitch the corners at an angle as shown.

5. Trim the back even with the quilt top. Turn the pillow cover to the right side. Insert the pillow form.

For quilt tops that measure larger than 16" x 16":
1. Follow steps 1 and 2 on page 28.
2. With right sides together, place the back pieces on the quilt top so that one edge of each piece is aligned with a raw edge of the quilt top and the opposite edge of each piece overlaps in the center. Fold back the overlapping edges, leaving a 4" overlap in the center. Press the folded edges under and hem them in place.

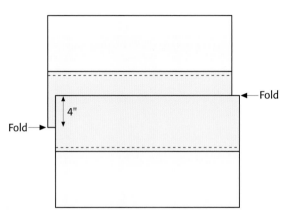

3. Follow steps 3–5 at left to finish the pillow cover.

Lattice Memories

By Gretchen K. Hudock, 11½" x 18½".

Technique: Straight borders and framing accents

Quick Bias is an easy way to create framing accents. Instead of piecing strips of fabric, just fuse Quick Bias in place. This little project will familiarize you with the basic techniques, and you'll end up with a special memory quilt, too. Use your favorite method for transferring photos to the fabric, or substitute some treasured pieces of needlework or rectangles cut from a special piece of fabric.

Materials

Yardage is based on 42"-wide fabric.

½ yd. fabric for background

½ yd. fabric for border and binding

½ yd. fabric for backing

3 yds. (approximately) Quick Bias

14" x 22" rectangle of batting

Three 4" x 6" photographs

Photo-transfer fabric and supplies

Temporary spray adhesive

Cutting

From the background fabric, cut:
1 rectangle, 12" x 20"

From the border and binding fabric, cut:
2 strips, each 5" x 42", for binding

Instructions

1. Refer to the manufacturer's instructions to transfer the photos to the photo-transfer fabric, leaving at least ¼" around each photo. Cut the photos from the fabric, leaving ⅛" around each photo if necessary to achieve a measurement of 4" x 6".

2. Mark the design lines on the right side of the background fabric as shown.

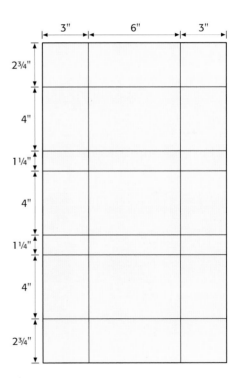

3. Follow the manufacturer's instructions to spray the wrong side of the fabric photos with temporary adhesive. Position the photos, right side up, in the 4" x 6" areas on the marked background fabric.

4. Refer to "Assembling the Project Layers" on page 17 to layer the quilt top with batting and backing.
5. Refer to "Applying the Quick Bias" on page 18 to fuse and stitch the Quick Bias over the center of the horizontal design lines; repeat with the vertical design lines. Use a ruler to keep the Quick Bias straight while you fuse it in place (see page 18).

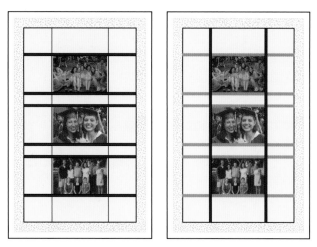

Apply horizontal bias strips first, then vertical strips.

6. To mark the border placement lines, measure the space between the Quick Bias at the bottom of the first photo and the top of the second photo. Add ¼" to this measurement. Measure this determined distance from the outside edge of both vertical strips of Quick Bias, and mark lines that extend the length of the background rectangle. Measure the determined distance from the outside edge of the top and bottom horizontal Quick Bias strips, and mark lines that extend the width of the background rectangle.

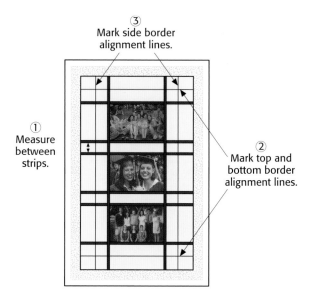

7. Refer to "Traditional Variation Method" on page 23 to cut the border strips 1¾" wide and apply them to the quilt top.
8. Refer to "French Twist Binding" on page 24 to bind the quilt edges.

Tic-Tac-Toe Twist

By Gretchen K. Hudock, 19" x 19".
Technique: Curved border embellishment

In this project, Quick Bias separates individual elements in the quilt top and creates a twined border embellishment. This small quilt would be a lovely accent in any room as a wall hanging or pillow. Use a fabric with preprinted vignettes that fit the room's decor, or refer to the instructions for "Lattice Memories" on page 30 to replace the vignettes with photos.

Materials

Yardage is based on 42"-wide fabric.

½ yd. fabric for background and outer border

¼ yd. fabric preprinted with vignettes approximately 3" square

½ yd. fabric for inner border and binding

¾ yd. fabric for backing

6½ yds. (approximately) Quick Bias

21" x 21" square of batting

¼ yd. sew-through paper-backed fusible web OR temporary spray adhesive

Cutting

From the background and outer border fabric, cut:
1 strip, 14" x 42". Crosscut to make:
    1 square, 14" x 14", for background
    4 strips, each 3½" x 21", for outer border

From the preprinted fabric, cut:
5 squares, each 3½" x 3½"

From the inner border and binding fabric, cut:
4 strips, each 1" x 21", for inner border
2 strips, 5" x 42", for binding

Instructions

1. Mark a 12½" x 12½" square in the center of the 14" x 14" background square. Mark the design inside the 12½" square as shown.

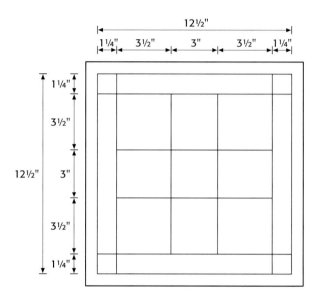

2. Follow the manufacturer's instructions for fusible web or spray adhesive to adhere the preprinted fabric squares temporarily to the background square in the positions shown. The center square will slightly overlap the other 4 squares.

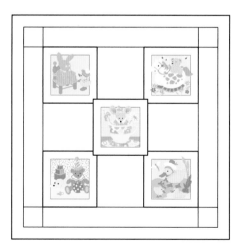

3. Refer to "Applying the Quick Bias" on page 18 to fuse and stitch the Quick Bias to the interior horizontal lines first, then to the interior vertical lines. Repeat with the exterior horizontal and vertical lines, extending the strips ¼" beyond the marked edge. Use a ruler to keep the Quick Bias straight while you fuse it in place (see page 18).

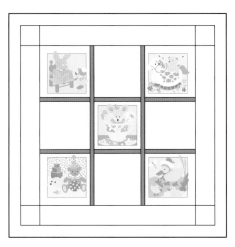

Apply interior horizontal bias strips,
then interior vertical strips.

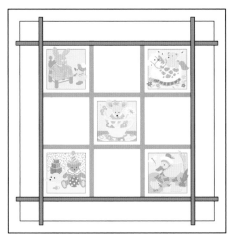

Apply exterior horizontal bias strips,
then exterior vertical strips.
Extend strips ¼" beyond marked edge.

4. Trim the quilt top to 12½" x 12½", keeping the design area centered.

5. With right sides together, stitch each 1" x 21" inner border to a 3½" x 21" outer border.

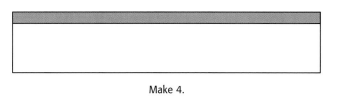

Make 4.

6. Measure and mark the center of each side of the quilt top. Mark the ¼" seam intersections on the 4 quilt corners.

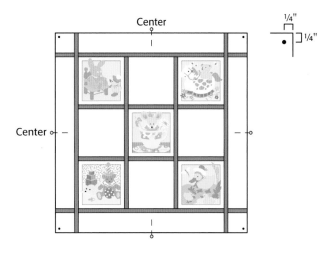

7. Measure and mark the center of each border, and also ¼" in from where the corners of the quilt will be. The borders are cut oversize, so you will need to measure the quilt through its vertical and horizontal centers to determine where the quilt corners will be.

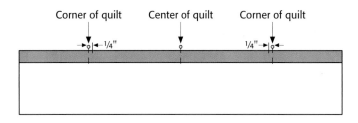

8. With right sides together, pin the side borders to the quilt top, matching center and corner marks. Stitch from corner mark to corner mark. Press the seam allowances toward the borders. Repeat for the top and bottom borders, making sure the stitching lines meet exactly at the corners.

9. With right sides together, fold the quilt diagonally so that the borders are aligned. Using a ruler with a 45° angle, draw a line on the wrong side of one of the borders from the corner mark to the outside corner as shown.

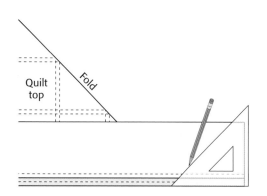

10. Pin the borders together and stitch on the drawn line. Open the top and make sure the seam is flat and accurate. Trim the seam allowances; then press it open. Repeat for the remaining corners.

11. Refer to "Transferring the Design to the Base Material" on page 12 to transfer the border design on page 38 to the outer border, adjusting the fit if necessary.

12. Refer to "Assembling the Project Layers" on page 17 to layer the quilt top with batting and backing.

13. Stitch in the ditch around the vignette squares and along the inside edge of the inner border. Quilt the plain blocks as desired. Refer to "Applying the Quick Bias" on page 18 to fuse the Quick Bias to the outer border in the order shown. Stitch the tape in place after all of the Quick Bias has been fused.

14. Refer to "French Twist Binding" on page 24 to bind the quilt edges.

Tip

When applying two layers of Quick Bias one on top of the other, you can choose to stitch each layer independently or wait until both layers are applied and then stitch. Remember, if you do the first, to leave the point of intersection on the first layer unstitched so you can tuck the ends of the second layer underneath to hide them. Planning ahead saves reverse sewing later!

First Application

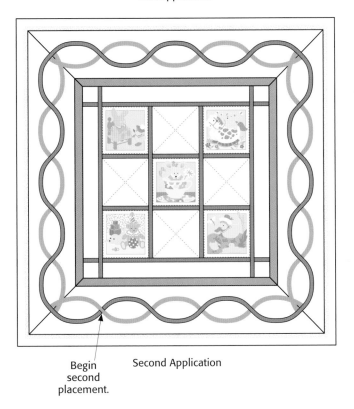

Begin second placement.

Second Application

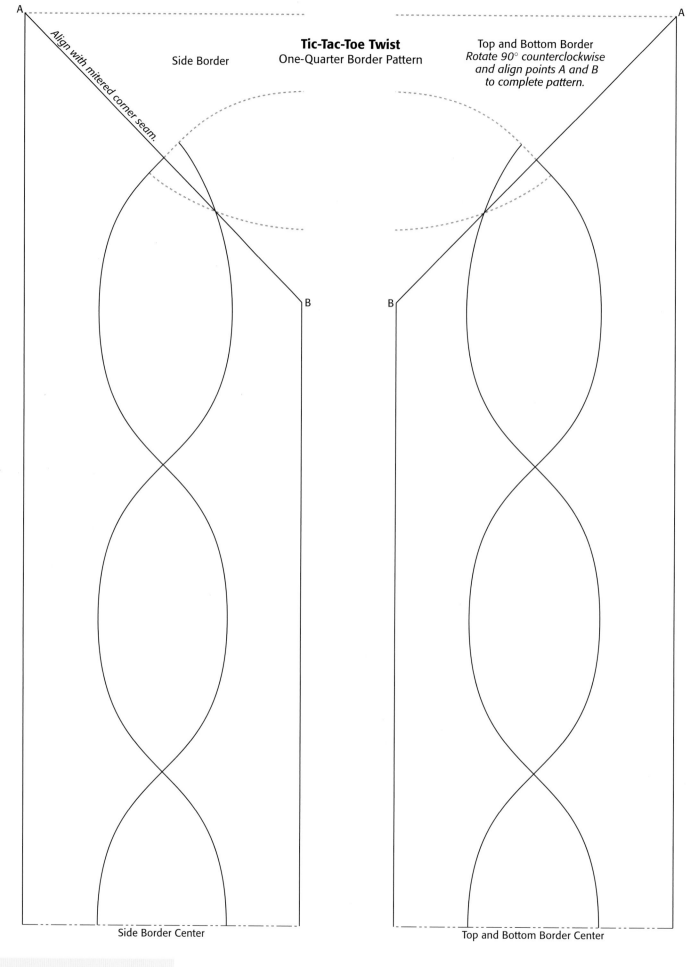

Tic-Tac-Toe Twist
One-Quarter Border Pattern

Side Border

Align with mitered corner seam.

Top and Bottom Border
*Rotate 90° counterclockwise
and align points A and B
to complete pattern.*

A

B

B

A

Side Border Center

Top and Bottom Border Center

I'm Bias for Spiders

By Gretchen K. Hudock, 17" x 17"; quilted by Mary Kotek.

Technique: Creating a design with quilting stencils

This spiderweb quilt will add a fun accent to the Halloween season. Once you've made one, you'll want to make more for gifts. The technique used in this project will work with many of the available quilting stencils. Just trace the design and add Quick Bias. No additional quilting is necessary, but you may wish to quilt in some more webs. The spiders are the creative addition of my coworker Sue. She decided that the web looked empty; so, with the help of a few button bodies and thread legs, the quilt is complete. This is one spiderweb you won't mind having in your house!

Materials

Yardage is based on 42"-wide fabric.

½ yd. fabric for background

¼ yd. fabric for inner and outer borders

⅝ yd. fabric for middle border and binding

⅝ yd. fabric for backing

3 yds. (approximately) Quick Bias

20" x 20" square of batting

3 black ⅜"-diameter shank buttons

2 black ⅝"-diameter shank buttons

Black all-purpose thread

Cutting

From the background fabric, cut:
1 square, 14" x 14"

From the inner and outer border fabric, cut:
4 strips, each 1" x 42"

From the binding fabric, cut:
2 strips, each 5" x 42". Set aside the remaining fabric to use for the middle border.

Instructions

1. Refer to "Transferring the Design to the Base Material" on page 12 to transfer the spiderweb design on page 42 to the 14" x 14" square of background fabric.

2. Refer to "Assembling the Project Layers" on page 17 to layer the background square with batting and backing.

3. Refer to "Applying the Quick Bias" on page 18 to fuse and stitch the Quick Bias to each curved ring of the web. Clip the tape at each point of the web to eliminate bulk.

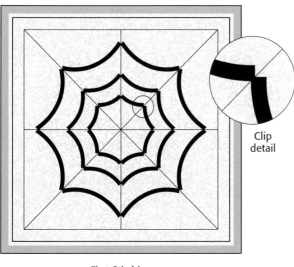

Clip detail

First Stitching

4. Apply and stitch the Quick Bias to the horizontal and vertical lines, extending the tape ¼" beyond the marked border line. Repeat for the diagonal lines.

Second Stitching

Third Stitching

5. Press the 1" x 42" inner and outer border strips in half lengthwise, wrong sides together. Refer to "Traditional Variation Method" on page 23 to cut the side inner borders the required length. Align raw edges with the marked border line. Stitch the borders to the quilt top, using a ³⁄₁₆" seam allowance, or move your needle one position to the right. Do not press the borders out. Repeat for the top and bottom inner borders.

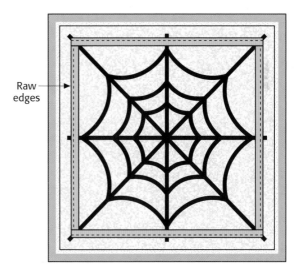

Raw edges

6. Referring to "Traditional Variation Method" on page 23, cut the middle borders 3" wide and sew them to the quilt top, using a ¼" seam allowance and aligning the inner and middle border raw edges. Press the borders out.

7. Using the remaining pressed 1" x 42" strips and referring to step 5, cut and sew the outer borders to the quilt top.

8. Add any quilting desired.

9. To make the spiders, sew the buttons in place where desired. Thread a hand-sewing needle with the black thread and knot the thread ends. Beginning at the shank each time, make 8 long stitches that extend past the button edge for the spider legs.

10. Refer to "French Twist Binding" on page 24 to bind the quilt edges.

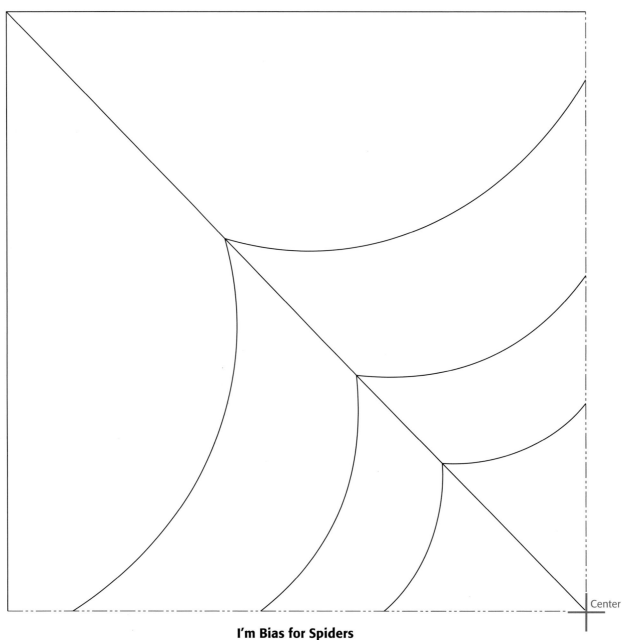

I'm Bias for Spiders
One-Quarter Pattern

Crown Jewel

By Gretchen K. Hudock, 18" x 18".

Technique: Converting traditional block designs into Quick Bias quilts

The traditional quilt blocks that we all cherish take on a new perspective with Quick Bias. And they come out perfect every time because no piecing is required! For this quilt, you'll learn to work with gridded fusible interfacing. The grid is already marked for you, so you just follow the lines to create the design, cut the fabric pieces to fit, press them in place, and apply the Quick Bias. Easy!

Materials

Yardage is based on 42"-wide fabric.

⅞ yd. solid or small print for background and binding

¼ yd. coordinating print

⅛ yd. coordinating solid or small print

¾ yd. fabric for backing

6½ yds. (approximately) Quick Bias

⅝ yd. gridded fusible interfacing with 1" squares

22" x 22" square of batting

Fine-point permanent marker

Cutting

From the background and binding fabric, cut:
1 square, 7" x 7", for center square
1 strip, 1¾" x 42", for parallelograms
2 strips, each 2¼" x 14", for side borders
2 strips, each 2¼" x 18½", for top and bottom borders
2 strips, each 5" x 42", for binding

From the coordinating print, cut:
2 squares, each 3½" x 3½"; cut each square in half once diagonally to yield 4 half-square triangles
1 square, 7" x 7"; cut in half twice diagonally to yield 4 quarter-square triangles

From the coordinating solid or small print, cut:
2 squares, each 3½" x 3½"; cut each square in half once diagonally to yield 4 half-square triangles

From the gridded fusible interfacing, cut:
1 square, 22" x 22"

Instructions

1. Fold the 1¾" x 42" background strip in half widthwise, wrong sides together. Using a ruler with a 45° angle, cut 2½"-wide segments as shown. Make 8 parallelograms.

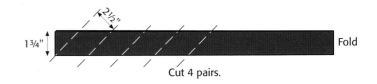

2. Tape the gridded fusible interfacing to the work surface, fusible side down, so it is taut.

3. Using a fine-point permanent marker, center and draw a 14" square on the smooth side of the fusible interfacing. Measuring from the upper left and lower right corners, mark the square at intervals of 3½", 7", and 10½", and connect the points as shown. Mark the remaining lines as shown to complete the pattern. Make sure the lines are dark enough to be seen from the fusible side of the interfacing.

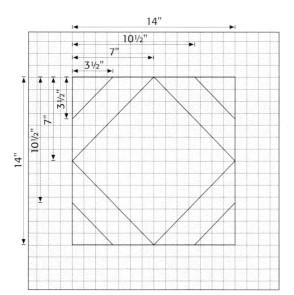

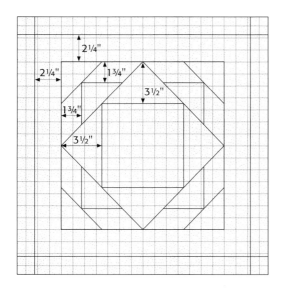

4. Remove the tape from the fusible interfacing. Position the fusible interfacing, fusible side up, on a padded pressing surface. Place the fabric pieces, right side up, in the positions shown, working from the center outward. Press the fabric pieces in place, being careful not to let the iron touch the interfacing.

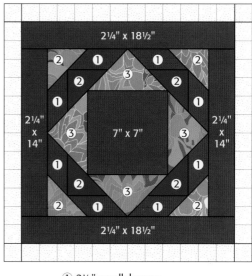

① 2½" parallelogram
② 3½" half-square triangle
③ 7" quarter-square triangle

5. Refer to "Transferring the Design to the Base Material" on page 12 to transfer the design on page 47 to the 7" x 7" center square.

6. Refer to "Assembling the Project Layers" on page 17 to layer the top with batting and backing.

7. Refer to "Applying the Quick Bias" on page 18 to fuse and stitch the Quick Bias to the design in the order shown on page 46. When applying the Quick Bias to the border "seams," fuse and stitch the vertical strips first, then the horizontal strips, extending the Quick Bias ¼" beyond the marked lines.

First Stitching

Crown Jewel II by Sue Petruske, 18" x 18". Sue used a featherstitch to attach the Quick Bias, giving it additional texture. It almost looks like a braid! Sue also chose to stitch the center of the design rather than highlight it with Quick Bias.

Second Stitching

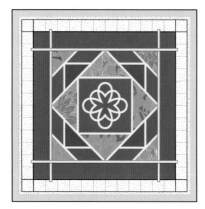

Third Stitching
Apply vertical bias strips,
then horizontal strips.

Tip

Remember to tuck under the starting point of the second layer of Quick Bias in the center design. Either remove stitches or leave an intersection unstitched in the first layer so you can tuck the end under.

8. Add any quilting desired.
9. Trim the backing, batting, and fusible web even with the edges of the quilt top.
10. Refer to "French Twist Binding" on page 24 to bind the quilt edges.

Crown Jewel
Pattern

Floral-Go-Round

By Gretchen K. Hudock, 16" x 16".
Technique: Circular designs

This project was developed for a class in circular designs. The simple curved shapes are easy to follow with Quick Bias, and the small size of the project makes it perfect for the center of a table or as a door decoration.

Materials

Yardage is based on 42"-wide fabric.

½ yd. fabric for background

¼ yd. multicolor print

⅛ yd. each of light solid and dark solid that coordinate with multicolor print

½ yd. fabric for backing

5½ yds. (approximately) Quick Bias

18" x 18" square of batting

½ yd. sew-through paper-backed fusible web OR temporary spray adhesive

Scrap of paper-backed fusible web

Cutting

From the background fabric, cut
1 square, 18" x 18"

Instructions

1. Refer to "Transferring the Design to the Base Material" on page 12 to transfer the design on page 53 to the 18" x 18" square of background fabric.

2. Referring to "Applying Fabric to the Marked Design" on page 15, use the patterns on page 52 to cut out and apply the fabric pieces to the marked design. Use either paper-backed fusible web or temporary spray adhesive. From the multicolor print fabric, cut 1 piece with pattern A and 4 pieces each with patterns D and E. From the light solid fabric, cut 2 pieces each with patterns B and C. From the dark solid fabric, cut 8 pieces with pattern F.

3. Refer to "Assembling the Project Layers" on page 17 to layer and pin-baste the top with batting only; the backing will be added later.

4. Refer to "Applying the Quick Bias" on page 18 to fuse and stitch the Quick Bias to the design in the order shown. When applying the Quick Bias to the straight outer lines, fuse and stitch the top, bottom, and straight side pieces first, then the diagonal side pieces. On the center circle, overlap the ends, turning under the top end to finish the raw edge.

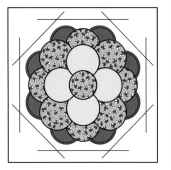

First Stitching

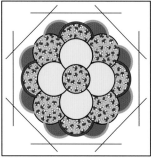

Second Stitching

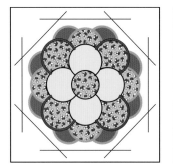

Third Stitching

Fourth Stitching

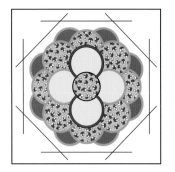

Fifth Stitching

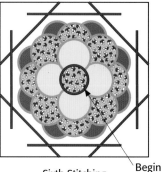

Sixth Stitching

Begin here.

5. Trim the excess fabric and batting 1" from the outer edge of the Quick Bias. Stitch a scant ¼" from the outer edges.

Scant ¼"

1"

6. With right sides together, center and pin the quilt top over the backing. Stitch completely around the quilt top, ¼" from the quilt-top outer edges. Trim the backing even with the quilt top; cut the seam allowance diagonally at each corner and trim the batting close to the stitching.

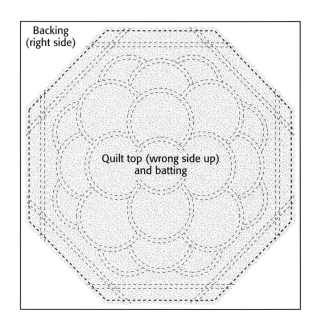

Backing (right side)

Quilt top (wrong side up) and batting

7. Cut a small slit in the center of the quilt backing, being careful not to cut the quilt top. Turn the project to the right side through the opening. Press.

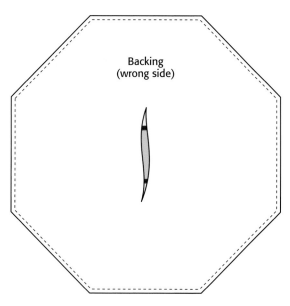

8. Cut a piece of backing fabric large enough to cover the opening. Follow the manufacturer's instructions to fuse the fusible web to the backing piece and apply it over the opening.

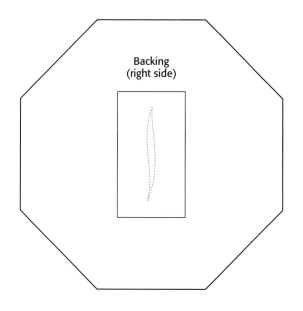

9. Stitch in the ditch around all of the Quick Bias edges.

Floral-Go-Round
Patterns

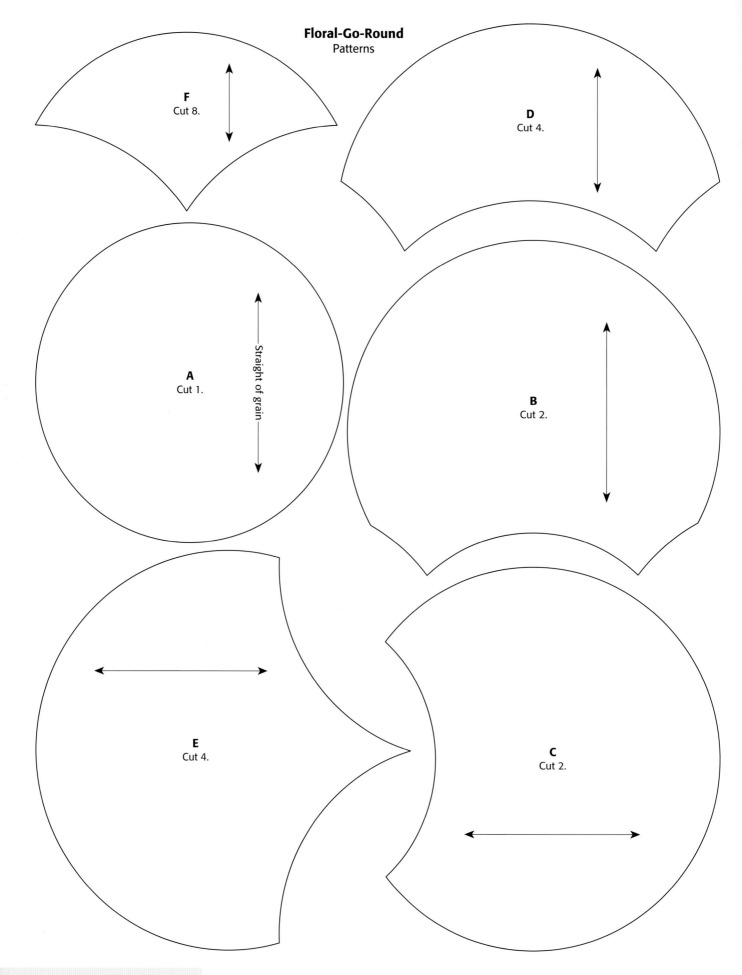

F
Cut 8.

D
Cut 4.

A
Cut 1.

Straight of grain

B
Cut 2.

E
Cut 4.

C
Cut 2.

Floral-Go-Round
One-Quarter Base Pattern

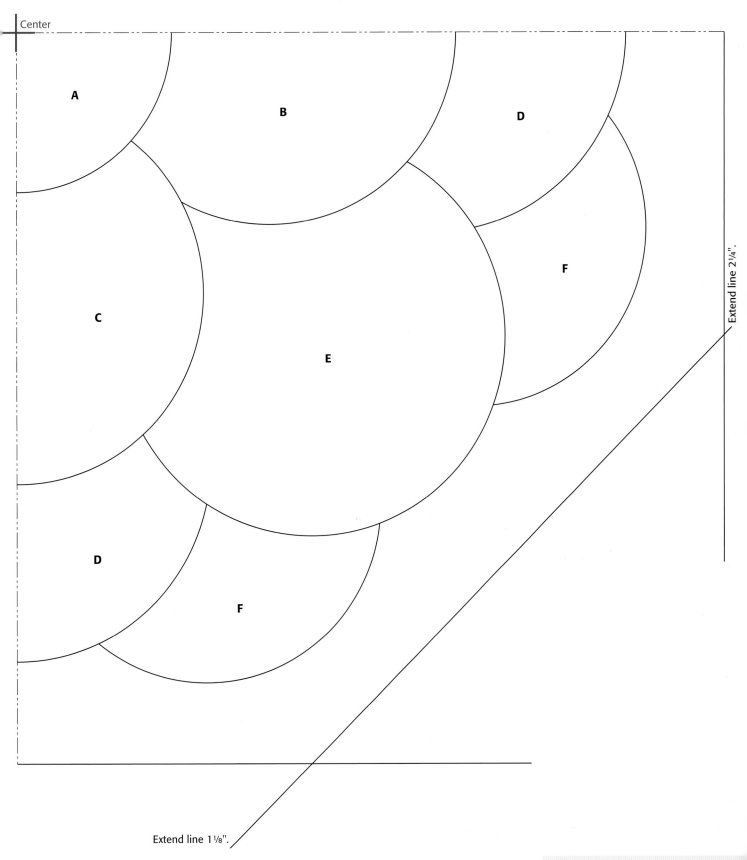

Center

A

B

D

C

E

F

D

F

Extend line 2¼".

Extend line 1⅛".

Cathedral Classico

By Gretchen K. Hudock, 15" x 36".

Technique: Circular design variation

Graceful curves give quiet elegance to this project. It is designed as a table runner, with a traditional binding for the edges. If you'd like to use the quilt as a wall hanging for a narrow wall, bind the edges using the French twist binding method on page 24. Consider also using the center design as a border treatment for a larger quilt.

Materials

Yardage is based on 42"-wide fabric.

½ yd. fabric for background

⅛ yd. small print for inner border

½ yd. fabric for outer border and binding

½ yd. fabric for backing

9½ yds. (approximately) Quick Bias

18" x 40" rectangle of batting

1 yd. sew-through paper-backed fusible web OR temporary spray adhesive

Cutting

From the small print, cut:
2 strips, each 1½" x 28", for side inner borders
2 strips, each 1½" x 10", for top and bottom inner borders

From the outer border and binding fabric, cut:
2 strips, each 2½" x 31", for side outer borders
2 strips, each 2½" x 15", for top and bottom outer borders
3 strips, each 2½" x 42", for binding

Instructions

1. Enlarge the design on page 57 to 200 percent. Refer to "Transferring the Design to the Base Material" on page 12 to trace the enlarged design onto the center of the background fabric.
2. Refer to "Assembling the Project Layers" on page 17 to layer the quilt top with batting and backing.
3. Refer to "Applying the Quick Bias" on page 18 to fuse and stitch the Quick Bias to the curved design lines in the order shown.

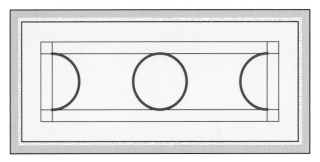

First Stitching

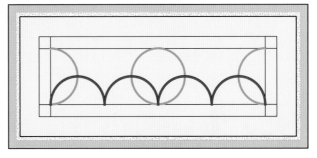

Second Stitching

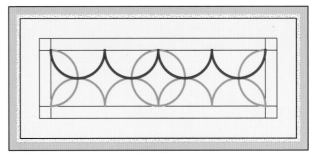

Third Stitching

4. Refer to "Quick Bias Method" on page 24 to apply the inner and outer borders, using either paper-backed fusible web or temporary spray adhesive. Apply the Quick Bias to the borders in the order shown, referring to the design pattern and the photograph on page 54 for the inner border short strips which meet the design points.

5. Add any quilting desired.
6. Referring to "French Twist Binding" on page 24, stitch the binding strips to the quilt edges. Fold the binding over the edges to the quilt back, covering the seam allowances and the stitching line. Stitch the binding in place along the seam line, mitering the corners. You will not be creating an opening to insert hanging rods.

First Stitching

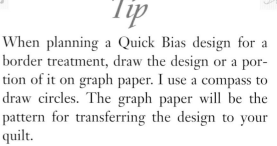

Tip

When planning a Quick Bias design for a border treatment, draw the design or a portion of it on graph paper. I use a compass to draw circles. The graph paper will be the pattern for transferring the design to your quilt.

If the border design is too large to fit on a sheet of graph paper, make a smaller drawing to scale and enlarge it to the correct size on a photocopy machine.

Second Stitching

Third Stitching

Cathedral Classico
One-Half Pattern

Enlarge to 200 percent.

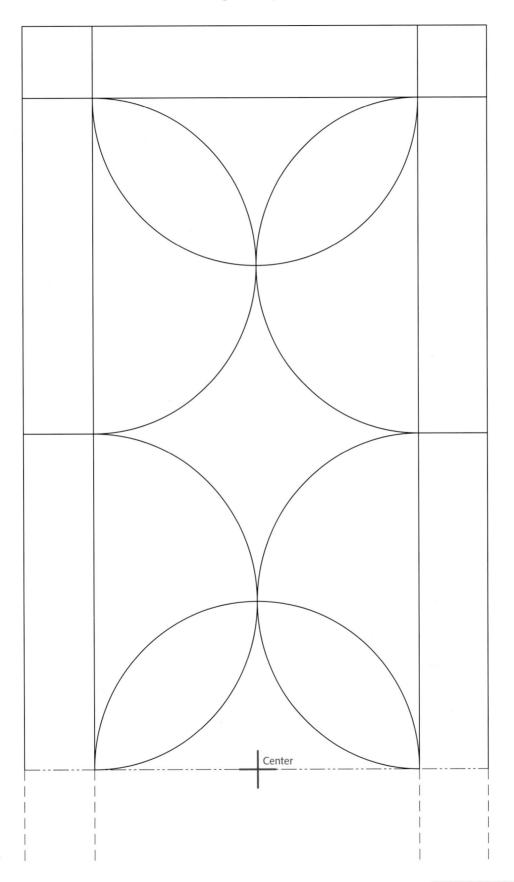

Center

Rainbow Baskets

By Gretchen K. Hudock, 22½" x 22½"; quilted by Mary Kotek.

Technique: Incorporating Quick Bias into pieced designs

The creation of rainbow-colored Quick Bias opened a new area of design possibilities. Used in one continuous piece, rainbow Quick Bias gives wonderful color gradation to a project; cutting it apart into individual color units is a way to be creative with color placement. In the traditional pieced Basket blocks of this quilt, individual color sections of Quick Bias simplified the appliqué handles. A black background fabric makes the rich colors of the rainbow Quick Bias stand out.

Materials

Yardage is based on 42"-wide fabric.

2¼ yds. black for background, inner and outer borders, and binding

⅛ yd. *each* of 5 fabrics in assorted colors that blend with Quick Bias for Basket blocks and border corner squares

¾ yd. fabric for backing

5½ yds. (approximately) rainbow-colored Quick Bias

26" x 26" square batting

Tear-away stabilizer

Template plastic

Cutting

From the black, cut:
2 strips, each 1¾" x 42"; crosscut to make:
    10 rectangles, each 1¾" x 3", for Basket blocks
    5 squares, each 1¾" x 1¾", for Basket blocks
4 squares, each 5½" x 5½", for plain blocks
5 squares, each 4¼" x 4¼", for Basket blocks
5 squares, each 2½" x 2½", for Basket blocks
3 strips, each 5" x 42", for binding

From *each* of 4 of the 5 assorted-color fabrics, cut:
1 square, 4¼" x 4¼", for Basket blocks
1 square, 3" x 3", for outer border corner squares
1 square, 2½" x 2½", for Basket blocks

From the remaining assorted-color fabric, cut:
1 square, 4¼" x 4¼", for Basket block
1 square, 2½" x 2½", for Basket block
4 squares, each 1¾" x 1¾", for inner border corner squares

Instructions

1. To make the basket handle squares, trace the basket handle placement pattern on page 62 onto template plastic; cut it out. Place the template on the right side of a black 4¼" square, aligning the corners and edges. Mark the curved side of the template onto the square. Repeat with the remaining black 4¼" squares.

2. From the Quick Bias, cut five 5" segments for the basket handles. Cut the segments from sections of the Quick Bias that coordinate with the colors of the basket fabrics. Place a piece of stabilizer under the marked curve on the black 4¼" squares. Refer to "Applying the Quick Bias" on page 18 to fuse and stitch the Quick Bias segment over the curved portion of the marked line on each square, extending the bias tape ¼" below the line. Tear away the stabilizer.

3. On the wrong side of each of the 5 assorted-color 4¼" squares, mark a diagonal line from corner to corner. With right sides together, place each marked assorted square over a black square from step 2 as shown.

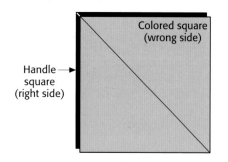

4. Stitch each pair of squares together along the marked diagonal line. Cut the blocks apart ¼" below the stitched line. Press the seam allowances open. Set the blocks aside.

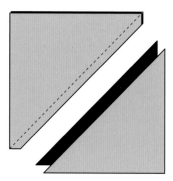

5. To make the basket base half-square triangles, mark a diagonal line from corner to corner on the wrong side of each of the assorted-color 2½" squares. Place each marked square on top of a black 2½" square, right sides together. Stitch ¼" away from both sides of the marked line. Cut the blocks apart on the marked line. Press the seam allowances open. Trim each square to 1¾" x 1¾".

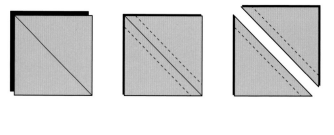

Trim to 1¾".
Make 5 pairs total.

6. To make the Basket blocks, stitch the basket handle square from step 1, 2 black 1¾" x 3" rectangles, two 1¾" squares from step 5, and 1 black 1¾" square together as shown. Make sure the basket handle square and the base squares from step 5 are the same color. Press the seam allowances open. Make 5 total.

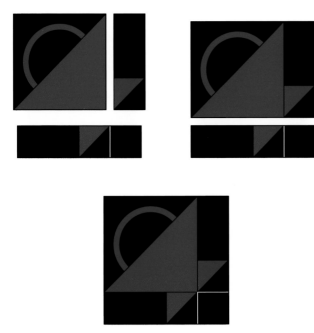

Make 5 total.

7. Stitch the Basket blocks and black 5½" squares together into 3 rows of 3 blocks each, alternating the position of the blocks in each row and placing the colors as shown. Press the seam allowances open.

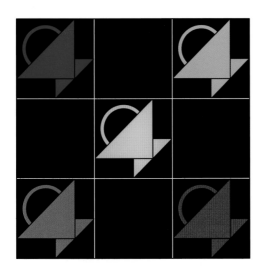

8. To make the inner borders, measure the quilt top through both the vertical center and the horizontal center. Cut 2 strips for each measurement, each 1¾" wide by the measurement. The strips cut to the vertical measurement will be for the side borders; the strips cut to the horizontal measurement will be for the top and bottom borders.

9. With right sides together, stitch a side inner border strip to each side of the quilt top. Press the seam allowances open. Stitch the four 1¾" squares of the same color to each end of the top and bottom inner border strips. Press the seam allowances open. Stitch the top and bottom border strips to the top and bottom edges of the quilt top. Press the seam allowances open.

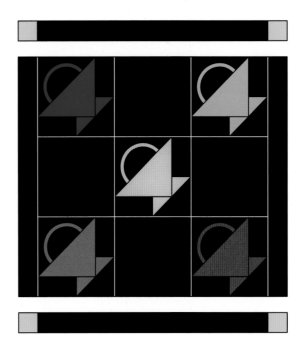

10. Refer to "Applying the Quick Bias" on page 18 to fuse and stitch Quick Bias to the border along the seam lines. The bias tape should butt up against the outer edge of the seam lines, not be centered over them. Apply the vertical pieces first and then the horizontal pieces.

11. Repeat steps 8 and 9 to attach the outer borders and apply the Quick Bias, using the 4 assorted-color 3" squares on the top and bottom border strip ends. Plan the placement of the assorted-color squares so each one is in the corner opposite the Basket block of the same color.

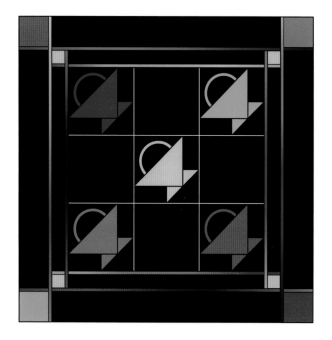

12. Refer to "Assembling the Project Layers" on page 17 to layer the quilt top with backing and batting.
13. Quilt diagonal lines through each of the plain squares to form an X, or quilt as desired.
14. Refer to "French Twist Binding" on page 24 to bind the quilt edges.

Rainbow Baskets
Handle Placement Pattern

Spiral Medallion

By Gretchen K. Hudock, 24" x 24"; quilted by Mary Kotek.

Technique: Stained glass quilts

Fabric designers have created fabrics with the swirls and shading of stained glass, enabling us to create home accessories with fabric and Quick Bias instead of glass and lead. Now, making stained glass quilts is easier than ever.

Materials

Yardage is based on 42"-wide fabric.

¾ yd. light print or solid for background

⅞ yd. dark solid for outer row of petals, outer border, and binding

¼ yd. multicolor print for middle row of petals

¼ yd. medium-color print for inner row of petals and inner border

⅞ yd. fabric for backing

5½ yds. (approximately) Quick Bias

26" x 26" square of batting

¾ yd. sew-through paper-backed fusible web OR temporary spray adhesive

Cutting

From the light print or solid, cut:
1 square, 22" x 22", for background

From the dark solid, cut:
3 strips, each 2" x 42", for outer border
3 strips, each 5" x 42", for binding

From the medium-color print, cut:
2 strips, each 1" x 42", for inner border

Instructions

1. Refer to "Transferring the Design to the Base Material" on page 12 to trace the pattern on page 67 onto the 22" x 22" square of background fabric. Measure 1½" from the side outer petals and the top and bottom outer petals, and mark the border lines as shown.

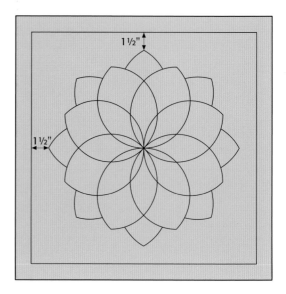

Tip

To make the tracing process easier, make two copies of the partial pattern on page 67 and tape them together along the dashed lines.

2. Refer to "Assembling the Project Layers" on page 17 to layer the marked top with batting and backing.

3. Referring to "Applying Fabric to the Marked Design" on page 15 and using the patterns on page 66, cut out 8 pieces each with patterns A, B, and C. Cut the A pieces from the dark solid, the B pieces from the multicolor print, and the C pieces from the medium print.

4. Apply the A pieces to the marked design. Refer to "Applying the Quick Bias" on page 18 to fuse and stitch the Quick Bias to the outer edge of each A piece as shown. Apply the B and C pieces to the marked design. Fuse and stitch the Quick Bias to the pieces as shown, using one continuous piece.

5. Refer to "Traditional Variation Method" on page 23 to cut the 1" x 42" inner borders to the correct length. Stitch the inner borders to the quilt top. Repeat to cut and stitch the 2" x 42" outer borders to the quilt top.

6. Add any quilting desired.

7. Refer to "French Twist Binding" on page 24 to bind the quilt edges.

Start here.

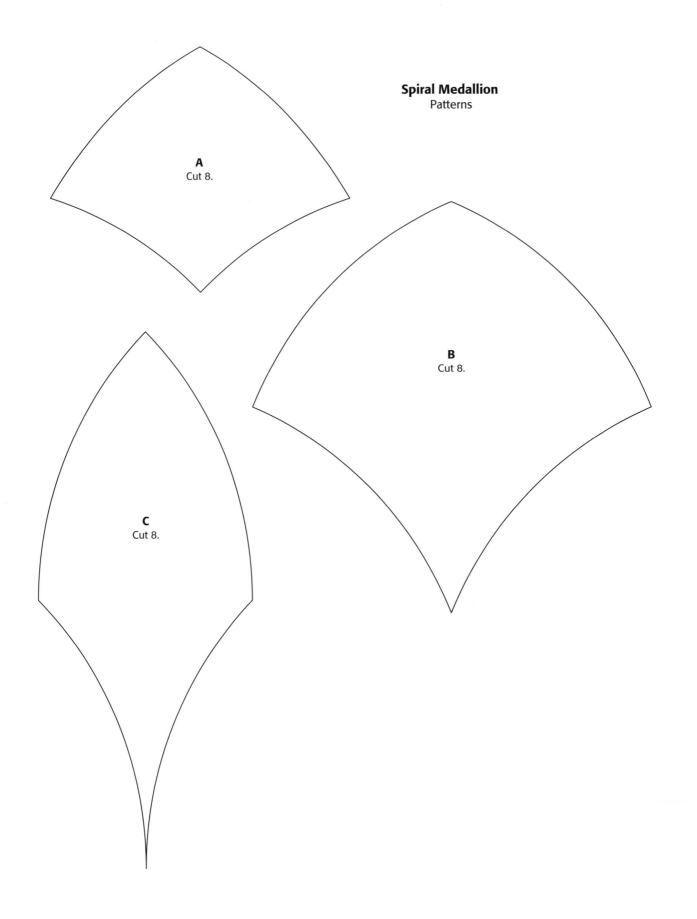

Spiral Medallion
Patterns

A
Cut 8.

B
Cut 8.

C
Cut 8.

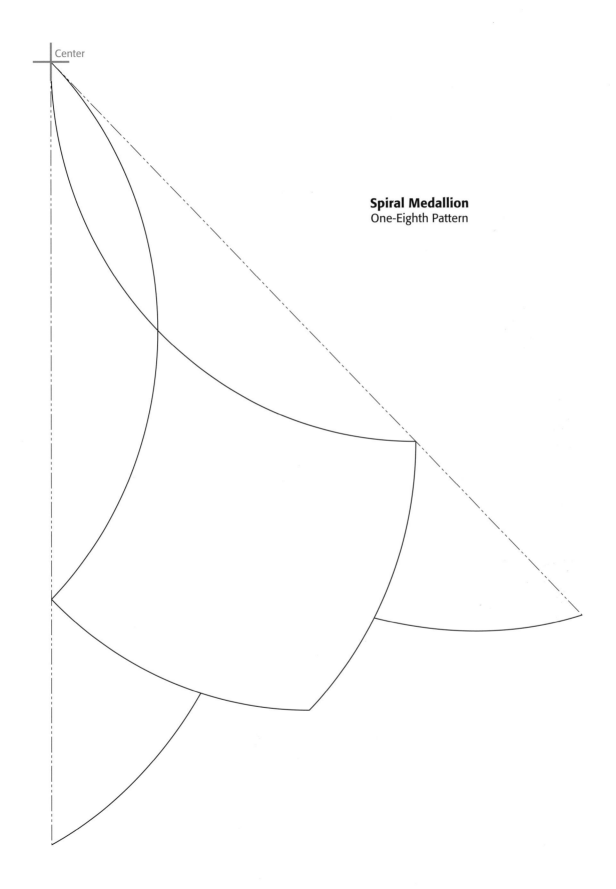

Center

Spiral Medallion
One-Eighth Pattern

Simply Seminole

By Sue Petruske, 20½" x 20½".

Technique: Streamlined Seminole piecing

This Southwestern-style table topper follows traditional Seminole piecing by stitching together strips of various widths and then recutting the strips at an angle. Here, Quick Bias creates the 1/4"-wide accent pieces that would ordinarily be difficult to piece. To make identifying the pieces easier, we've called for the fabric colors used in the photographed project, but feel free to change them to suit your decor.

Materials

Yardage is based on 42"-wide fabric.

1/4 yd. gold print for Seminole strips and center square borders

3/4 yd. dark blue print for center square, Seminole strips, and binding

1/4 yd. dark blue solid for Seminole strips

7/8 yd. fabric for backing

5 1/2 yds. (approximately) Quick Bias

24" x 24" square of batting

Cutting

From the gold print, cut:
3 strips, each 2" x 42", for Seminole strips
2 strips, each 2" x 6 1/2", for center square side borders
2 strips, each 2" x 9 1/2", for center square top and bottom borders

From the dark blue print, cut:
3 strips, each 2" x 42", for Seminole strips
1 square, 6 1/2" x 6 1/2", for center square
2 strips, each 2 1/2" x 42", for binding

From the dark blue solid, cut:
2 strips, each 3" x 42", for Seminole strips
1 strip, 2" x 42", for Seminole strips

Instructions

1. With right sides together, stitch the gold print 2" x 6 1/2" side borders to the sides of the dark blue print 6 1/2" x 6 1/2" center square. Stitch the gold print 2" x 9 1/2" top and bottom borders to the top and bottom edges of the center square.

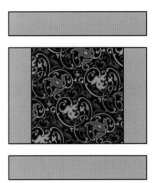

2. To make the Seminole strip sets for the side, top, and bottom edges of the center-square unit, stitch 1 gold print 2" x 42" strip, 1 dark blue print 2" x 42" strip, and 1 dark blue solid 3" x 42" strip right sides together as shown, staggering the ends 2" to the right with each addition. Repeat to make a second strip set, this time staggering the ends 2" to the left with each addition. Press the seam allowances open.

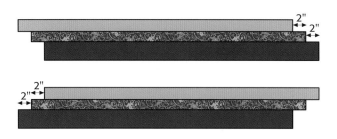

3. Refer to "Applying the Quick Bias" on page 18 to fuse and stitch the Quick Bias over the center of each seam line of both strip sets.

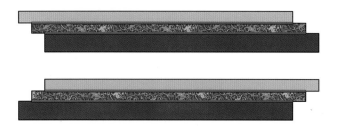

4. Trim one end of each strip set at a 45° angle as shown. Measuring from the cut edge, cut 12 strips from each strip set, each 2" wide.

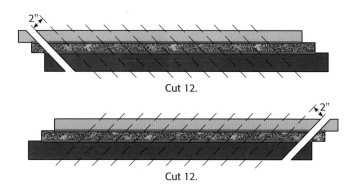

Cut 12.

Cut 12.

5. With right sides together, stitch a strip from one strip set to a strip from the other strip set, matching the Quick Bias ends. The strips should be mirror images of each other. Press the seam allowances open. Make 12.

Note: The strips are cut on the bias, so be careful not to stretch them while stitching and pressing.

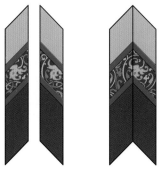

Make 12.

6. Sew 3 pairs of strips together. Press the seam allowances open. Make 4.

Make 4.

7. Trim the gold print end of the pieced strips ½" from the Quick Bias points as shown. Set the pieced strips aside.

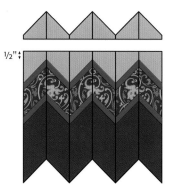

½"

8. To make the Seminole strip set for the corners of the center square unit, stitch the remaining gold print, dark blue print, and dark blue solid 2" x 42" strips right sides together, staggering the ends 2" to the left. Press the seam allowances open. Do not add the Quick Bias to these strips yet.

9. Trim the left end of the strip set at a 45° angle. To cut out the triangles, turn the ruler in the opposite direction and position it so the 45°-angle mark is aligned with the strip set lower edge and the ruler right edge is placed on the upper left corner of the strip set as shown. Cut along the ruler right edge. Continue alternating the direction of the ruler to cut out 7 triangles. Remove the 3 triangles that point down and set them aside for another project.

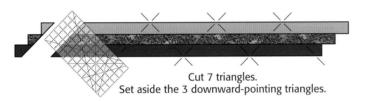

Cut 7 triangles.
Set aside the 3 downward-pointing triangles.

10. Refer to "Applying the Quick Bias" on page 18 to fuse and stitch the Quick Bias over the center of each seam line of the remaining 4 triangles.

11. Stitch a pieced strip set from step 7 to the top and bottom edges of the center-square unit. Stitch a pieced corner triangle to each side of the 2 remaining pieced strip sets as shown. Stitch the

pieced side units to each side of the center-square unit. Press the seam allowances open.

12. Trim the quilt top's jagged edges even with the corners.

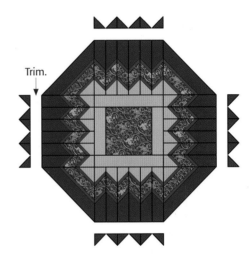

Trim.

13. Refer to "Assembling the Project Layers" on page 17 to layer the quilt top with batting and backing.
14. Quilt as desired.
15. Referring to "French Twist Binding" on page 24, stitch the binding strips to the quilt edges. Fold the binding over the edges to the quilt back, covering the seam allowance and the stitching line. Stitch the binding in place along the seam line, mitering the corners. You will not be creating an opening to insert a hanging rod.

Woven Trellis

By Gretchen K. Hudock, 28" x 28".

Technique: Using other designs as sources

Sashiko designs are another source for Quick Bias creations. According to Kitty Pippen's book, Quilting with Japanese Fabrics *(Martingale & Company, 2000), sashiko is a running stitch traditionally done in white thread on indigo-color fabric. Originally, sashiko was used to mend clothing, but we now use its beautiful designs in quilting. Here, the simple geometric shapes that make up a sashiko basket-weave pattern give you an easy grid for your work. It is not necessary to restrict yourself to Japanese-inspired fabrics in this design, but their richness and style marry beautifully with Quick Bias. This wall quilt is a good exercise in accuracy for the quilter who likes a challenge.*

Materials

Yardage is based on 42"-wide fabric.

⅞ yd. multicolor print for hexagons, outer border, and binding

¼ yd. *each* of 3 coordinating fabrics for trellis pieces

¼ yd. coordinating fabric for inner border

1 yd. fabric for backing

11 yds. (approximately) Quick Bias*

⅞ yd. gridded fusible interfacing with 1" squares

30" x 30" square of batting

*Because this design has many cuts, it is important not to leave an excessive amount of bias tape beyond each cutting point.

Cutting

From the multicolor print, cut:
1 strip, 4" x 42", for hexagons
3 strips, each 2" x 42", for outer border
3 strips, each 5" x 42", for binding

From *each* of the 3 coordinating fabrics, cut:
2 strips, 1⅞" x 42", for trellis pieces

From the inner border fabric, cut:
3 strips, each 1" x 42"

From the gridded fusible interfacing, cut:
1 square, 30" x 30"

Instructions

1. To make the hexagons, cut the end of the multicolor 4" x 42" strip at a 60° angle. Cut 7 segments, each 4" wide, along the 60° angle as shown. Measure 2" from the center point of each segment and cut off the ends to make the hexagons.

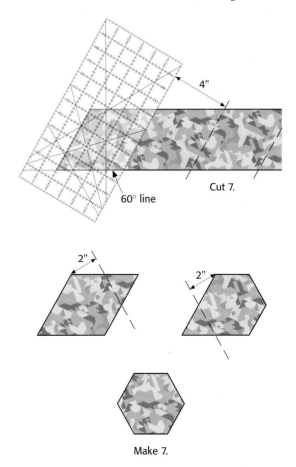

Make 7.

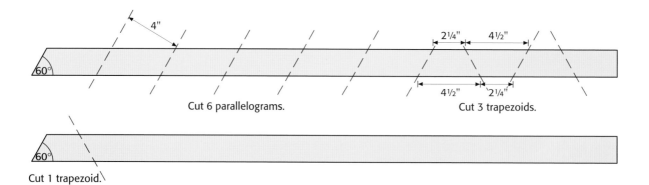

4"

60°

Cut 6 parallelograms.

2¼" 4½"

4½" 2¼"

Cut 3 trapezoids.

60°

Cut 1 trapezoid.

2. To make the trellis pieces, cut the end of each of the 6 coordinating-fabric 1⅞" x 42" strips at a 60° angle. From 1 strip of each fabric, cut 6 parallelograms, each 4" wide, along the 60° angle, and 3 trapezoids, each 2¼" along one edge and 4½" along the opposite edge, alternating the angle of each cut, as shown above. From each of the 3 remaining strips, cut 1 additional trapezoid.

3. Fold the interfacing in half lengthwise and widthwise to find the center; crease the center point.

4. Unfold the interfacing and place it, fusible side up, on a padded pressing surface. Center a hexagon piece, right side up, on the interfacing, aligning the top and bottom edges of the hexagon within the grid markings.

5. Begin placing the trellis pieces into position around the hexagon, referring to the photo on page 72 and using the grid lines for accuracy. Continue to add the hexagon and trellis pieces until the center design is complete. The Quick Bias will be added after all of the pieces are in place.

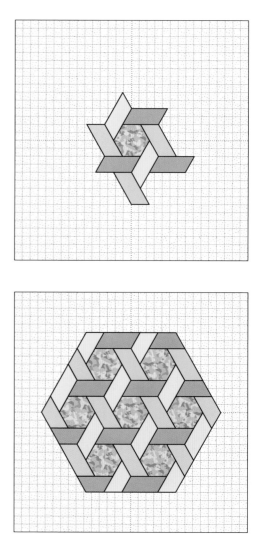

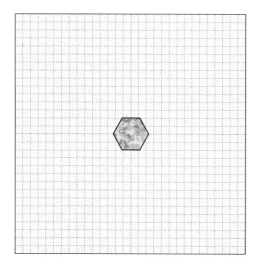

6. Press the fabric pieces in place, being careful not to let the iron touch the interfacing. Turn the piece over and press gently from the wrong side.

7. Turn the quilt top over to the fusible side. Position an inner border along every other edge of the quilt top. Trim the strips to fit. Repeat with the remainder of each strip on the remaining sides. Press the strips in place.

8. Repeat step 7 for the outer borders.

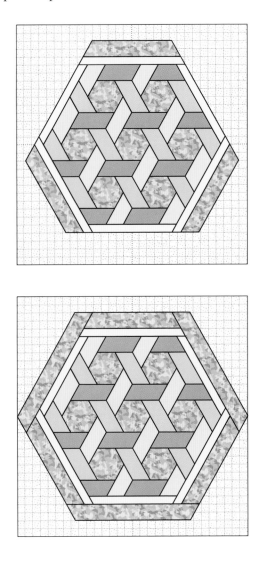

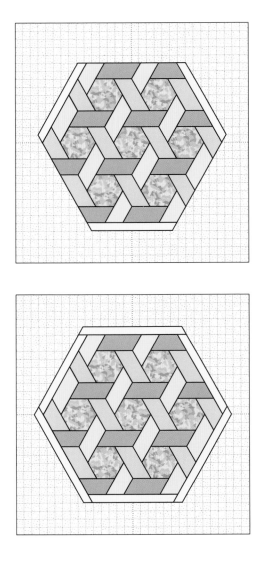

9. Refer to "Assembling the Project Layers" on page 17 to layer the quilt top with backing and batting.

10. Referring to "Applying the Quick Bias" on page 18 and the diagram below, fuse Quick Bias to the edges of each trellis strip in the order indicated. Use a ruler to keep the Quick Bias straight while you fuse it in place (see page 18). Do not stitch the pieces in place yet. Trim the end of the Quick Bias just beyond the point where another strip will cross over it. If the strip intersects a previously adhered strip, re-warm the area where the strips intersect and place the end of the new strip under the previously adhered strip. If the strip meets 2 other strips (these intersections are marked on the diagram with the number of the strip followed by an X), cut the end of the strip ¼" beyond the inner edge of the intersected strip that runs perpendicular to the new strip, re-warm the intersection, lift up the pressed-down strips at the intersection, and tuck the end of the new strip under them.

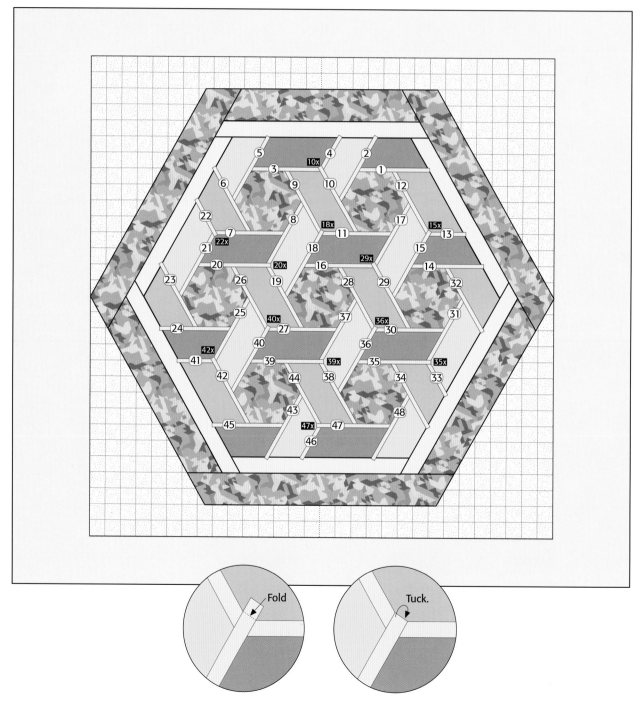

X Intersection Details

11. Once all of the Quick Bias is fused, stitch it down. It is helpful to stitch down the Quick Bias on one side of all the pieces, then on the other side.

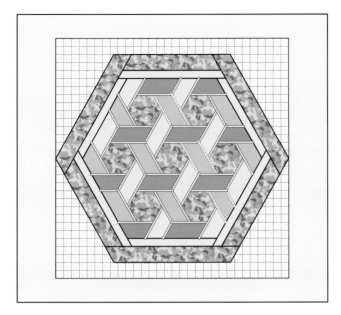

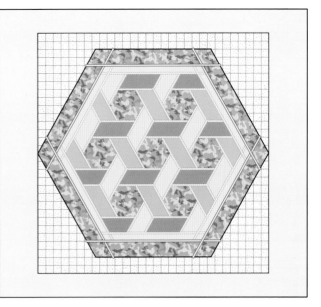

Outer Quick Bias Border

13. Add any quilting desired.
14. Refer to "French Twist Binding" on page 24 to bind the quilt edges.

12. Fuse Quick Bias to the inner edge of the inner border, extending the strips to the inner edge of the outer border. Stitch the Quick Bias in place, beginning with the inner edge. Repeat to apply Quick Bias to the inner edge of the outer border.

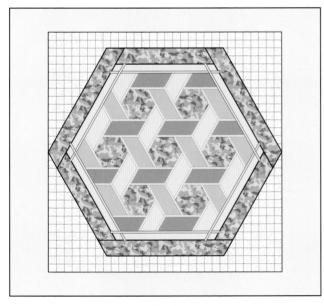

Inner Quick Bias Border

Resources

Connecting Threads
PO Box 8940
Vancouver, WA 98668-8940
800-574-6454
www.connectingthreads.com

Connecting Threads carries general quilting supplies as well as many of the specialized supplies required for the projects, including Quick Bias, a mini-iron, and a fusible-bias-tape maker.

Nancy's Notions
PO Box 683
333 Beichl Avenue
Beaver Dam, WI 53916-0683
800-833-0690
www.nancysnotions.com

Nancy's Notions carries all of the tools and notions needed for making the projects in this book.

About the Author

Gretchen K. Hudock began quilting in 1984 after watching a quilting show on public television. She began designing quilt patterns in 1989, and Christmas quilts soon became her specialty. Many of her holiday designs have been published nationally, and her *Christmas Card Quilts* led to a three-part series shown on public television's *Sewing with Nancy*. Since 1995, Gretchen has been the quilting consultant for Nancy's Notions, where she designs catalog projects, tests new products, and promotes quilting whenever possible. She lives in Slinger, Wisconsin, with her husband, Rich. They have two children, John and Elizabeth, who are both in college but occasionally come home to visit. The family dog, Waldo, tests and approves, and occasionally redesigns, each project.

new and bestselling titles from

America's Best-Loved Craft & Hobby Books®

America's Best-Loved Quilt Books®

NEW RELEASES
1000 Great Quilt Blocks
Basically Brilliant Knits
Bright Quilts from Down Under
Christmas Delights
Creative Machine Stitching
Crochet for Tots
Crocheted Aran Sweaters
Cutting Corners
Everyday Embellishments
Folk Art Friends
Garden Party
Hocus Pocus!
Just Can't Cut It!
Quilter's Home: Winter, The
Sweet and Simple Baby Quilts
Time to Quilt
Today's Crochet
Traditional Quilts to Paper Piece

APPLIQUÉ
Appliquilt in the Cabin
Artful Album Quilts
Artful Appliqué
Blossoms in Winter
Color-Blend Appliqué
Sunbonnet Sue All through the Year

BABY QUILTS
Easy Paper-Pieced Baby Quilts
Even More Quilts for Baby
More Quilts for Baby
Play Quilts
Quilted Nursery, The
Quilts for Baby

HOLIDAY QUILTS & CRAFTS
Christmas Cats and Dogs
Creepy Crafty Halloween
Handcrafted Christmas, A
Make Room for Christmas Quilts
Welcome to the North Pole

HOME DECORATING
Decorated Kitchen, The
Decorated Porch, The
Dresden Fan
Gracing the Table
Make Room for Quilts
Quilts for Mantels and More
Sweet Dreams

LEARNING TO QUILT
101 Fabulous Rotary-Cut Quilts
Beyond the Blocks
Casual Quilter, The
Feathers That Fly
Joy of Quilting, The
Simple Joys of Quilting, The
Your First Quilt Book (or it should be!)

PAPER PIECING
40 Bright and Bold Paper-Pieced Blocks
50 Fabulous Paper-Pieced Stars
For the Birds
Quilter's Ark, A
Rich Traditions
Split-Diamond Dazzlers

ROTARY CUTTING
365 Quilt Blocks a Year Perpetual Calendar
Around the Block Again
Around the Block with Judy Hopkins
Fat Quarter Quilts
More Fat Quarter Quilts
Stack the Deck!
Triangle Tricks
Triangle-Free Quilts

SCRAP QUILTS
Nickel Quilts
Scrap Frenzy
Scrappy Duos
Spectacular Scraps
Strips and Strings
Successful Scrap Quilts

TOPICS IN QUILTMAKING
American Stenciled Quilts
Americana Quilts
Batik Beauties
Bed and Breakfast Quilts
Fabulous Quilts from Favorite Patterns
Frayed-Edge Fun
Patriotic Little Quilts
Reversible Quilts

CRAFTS
ABCs of Making Teddy Bears, The
Blissful Bath, The
Handcrafted Frames
Handcrafted Garden Accents
Handprint Quilts
Painted Chairs
Painted Whimsies

KNITTING & CROCHET
365 Knitting Stitches a Year Perpetual
    Calendar
Clever Knits
Crochet for Babies and Toddlers
Crocheted Sweaters
Knitted Sweaters for Every Season
Knitted Throws and More
Knitter's Book of Finishing Techniques, The
Knitter's Template, A
More Paintbox Knits
Paintbox Knits
Too Cute! Cotton Knits for Toddlers
Treasury of Rowan Knits, A
Ultimate Knitter's Guide, The

Our books are available at bookstores and your favorite craft, fabric, and yarn retailers. If you don't see the title you're looking for, visit us at **www.martingale-pub.com** or contact us at:

1-800-426-3126

International: 1-425-483-3313

Fax: 1-425-486-7596

Email: info@martingale-pub.com

For more information and a full list of our titles, visit our Web site.